COMING TO JESUS

COMING TO JESUS

ONE MAN'S SEARCH FOR TRUTH AND LIFE PURPOSE

BRITT GILLETTE

DEDICATION

To my wife, Jen, devoted follower of Jesus Christ who has fought by my side through all of life's peaks and valleys. You are the love of my life, and you were instrumental in the creation of this book.

CONTENTS

CHAPTER 1
A SPIRITUAL VACUUM

"There is a God-shaped vacuum in the heart of every person, and it can never be filled by any created thing."

— Blaise Pascal

IN THE SPRING of 1992, I found myself alone in a hospital bed late at night. Through a cracked door, a dim light filtered into the room along with the muffled voices of the night shift staff. Wires from a nearby machine ran into my nose deep into my stomach, and I felt an eerie sense of isolation.

Two years earlier, I contracted encephalitis – a virus which causes swelling of the brain. I can't begin to describe the struggle involved in dealing with such an illness and its aftermath. Recovery was slow, yet steady, and life eventually returned to somewhat normal.

But it didn't return for long. Soon thereafter, I was struck with a mysterious gastrointestinal disease. And after months and months of testing, I found myself in the Children's Hospital for my latest procedure – an invasive esophageal pH test to measure acid reflux.

Needless to say, I couldn't sleep. It's not so easy to sleep with wires shoved up your nose. I just stared at the ceiling and counted the tiles, immersed in an empty feeling of loneliness which drained every last ounce of energy.

After months of testing, the doctors weren't any closer to finding an answer, and I didn't know what to expect next. While whatever I had didn't seem to be life threatening, it was definitely life altering. And at age 14, I began to ponder my own mortality. A number of questions entered my mind.

What if I died tonight? Other than my family and a few friends, would anyone care? Who would even know? And fifty years from now, if my parents are gone, who other than my brother and a handful of relatives will ever even know that I existed? A thousand years from now, will the world ever even know I lived?

The initial answers which formed in my mind were not very comforting, and a hollow realization took hold and wouldn't let go. While I didn't know it at the time, I had discovered the same God-shaped vacuum Pascal identified years before, only I didn't know what it was or how to fix it.

As a young child, I used to look in the mirror and feel it. It was a brief, yet dreadful feeling. I would just stare at myself and wonder, *"Who am I? Why do I exist, and why am I me?"* I couldn't stand to do it for more than a moment or two. While I was acutely aware that I was physically alive, I was spiritually dead – and I didn't know why. While I lived life and enjoyed life, I was really just going through the motions. I wasn't really ***living*** life. I wasn't conscious. I wasn't really awake, and I didn't ever question life's purpose.

Now those same dreadful feelings from the mirror returned as I lay in a strange bed in the late hours of the night with more and more questions.

If no one will ever know I lived, then what's the purpose? What's the point of life?

I'm sure you've pondered these same questions yourself, and probably at a much earlier age (hey, I never claimed to be the brightest kid in the class!) But for me, these were new questions, and I didn't like it one bit that I didn't have the answers.

Maybe you're experiencing these same feelings of emptiness right now, wandering through life with no purpose. Maybe you're overcome with feelings of anxiety and depression. If so, maybe my story can help you. Why? Because all those years ago, I woke up from life and made it my number one goal to find the truth – the truth about why I felt such intense feelings of emptiness, and more importantly, what I could do to eliminate them.

I set out to find answers to all of those questions. The same ones you've faced and pondered. *Who am I? Why do I exist? Why am I me? What's the purpose of my life? What happens when I die? Is there a God? And if there is a God, who is He? And does He care about me?*

So what did I find? I found the answers – ***every single one of them***, and my life has never been the same.

CHAPTER 2
SEARCHING FOR TRUTH

"'What is truth?' Pilate asked."

— John 18:38 (NLT)

GROWING UP MY parents didn't go to church. A few times, I attended church with my grandmother, and at least once I remember our family "trying out" a local church when one of our neighbors invited us, but to my knowledge we only attended one Sunday service and never returned.

Spiritual matters were rarely discussed, and I wasn't sure what my parents believed in regard to God, eternity, and the afterlife. In hindsight, this provided me with an enormous advantage. My search for truth began as a clean slate with no predisposition toward any particular philosophy or religion. I didn't have a predetermined allegiance or bias toward any particular religious doctrines or denominations. In fact, I had never given much thought to such things.

But now I did. I wanted answers. Not guesses, beliefs, or fairy tales. I wanted to know the true purpose of life, not just take up a hobby or set a goal. I wanted truth, and I was ready to explore every religion, philosophy, and library in order to find it.

Why? Not only did I want to know what was important in this world, but I also wanted to know what (if anything) would come next. After all, I made a simple observation which somehow goes unnoticed by an enormous number of people.

What is this simple observation?

You're going to die.

That's right. Rich or poor. Old or young. Powerful king or pacifist monk. It doesn't matter who you are. Sooner or later, you're going to die.

And while you wouldn't know it by listening to today's media, it doesn't matter if you eat right and exercise every day. Sure, it might extend your life a few years – maybe. But you know what?

You're still going to die.

And it doesn't matter how much fame or power or money you have. No matter how great you think you are or how much power you think you have...

You're going to die.

So it seemed quite reasonable to expect that one day I was going to die. The only thing I didn't know was **when** I was going die, not **whether** I would die.

Coming face to face with my own mortality, I could clearly see that no matter our lot in life, we all share the same destination. And given this certainty, it also seemed quite reasonable to prepare for my death and its immediate aftermath the same as I would for any future event, such as saving for retirement or planning a future career.

But I had a problem. How could I prepare for an unknown future? While death is certain, what happens after that?

I didn't know. Did anyone?

And even if someone *claimed* to know what happens after death, how do I prove them right or wrong?

I wanted answers, so I studied the Bible, the Koran, Confucius, Hinduism, Buddhism, and the writings of every philosopher and political and social leader I could get my hands on. And while many of these sources offered elements of truth, I faced the same problem. How could I really know for sure which (if any) of these sources offered the truth about reality.

The Bible, and more specifically, the words of Jesus seemed to make more sense than anything else I had read. Why? Jesus had a presence, even when reading about Him, which seemed "apart" from the world, and even people I knew who didn't believe in Jesus held in Him in reverence as a "great teacher."

But ultimately, I couldn't be sure about the Bible either. After all, conventional wisdom told me the Bible was an ancient collection of outdated writings based on man-made superstitions and fairy tales. While Christians claimed the Bible was the Word of God, how could I prove it one way or the other?

I couldn't, so I continued to explore. Then one day, I read a magazine article which referenced Hal Lindsey's best-selling 1970 book *The Late Great Planet Earth.* It sounded interesting, so I went to the book store at the local mall and purchased a copy. It was an eye-opening experience. Lindsey cited fulfilled prophecies made by Moses, Isaiah, Jeremiah, Daniel, Ezekiel, Amos, Jesus, and others. The specificity and accuracy of these prophecies was like nothing I had ever seen or heard of before.

But were they really true? Did the Bible really predict specific future events long before they took place? If so, this would be a major breakthrough in my search for truth. After all, if the Bible contained hundreds of specific prophecies written hundreds of years in advance of their fulfillment, while other books claiming divine origin did not, I would have a clear reason to accept the Bible's claims as true.

So now I had some investigating to do. **Did** other texts or people make the same or similar predictions? If so, then Hal Lindsey's claims about the Bible weren't so awe-inspiring. I considered this possibility and continued to examine the same books and writings as before, but this time with an eye on prophecy and future predictions. Here's what I found.

THE KORAN

The Koran. According to Muslims, it's the final revelation of God (Allah) given to man through the prophet Muhammad. Most people in the Western world don't know that Muslims consider Allah to be the god of the same

Abraham chronicled in the Old Testament, and they consider Moses and Jesus to be prophets (although they discount the Christian claim that Jesus is the Son of God).

So I approached the Koran with an open mind. After all, if fulfilled bible prophecy could prove the Bible had divine origins, perhaps similar prophecies could prove the Koran is the extension of God's Word as Muslims claim. So I set out to see if the Koran also contained numerous fulfilled prophecies.

The Koran is divided into 114 Suras (chapters), covering any number of subjects including what some claim are fulfilled prophecies of future events. Advocates point to more than sixty passages which they claim are prophetic in nature, but most of these passages are vague, ambiguous, and sometimes not even prophecies at all. If you have access to a Koran, go ahead and look at these passages for yourself. If not, you can easily find them on the Internet.

For instance, *Sura 4:119* is said to be a prediction of genetic engineering. But I think it's quite a stretch to say that cutting "the ears of cattle" and altering "Allah's creation" are clear and absolute predictions of human beings engaged in genetic engineering. Like many purported prophecies, this verse is vague in its prediction (assuming it's an attempted prediction at all).

Here's another example. Supposedly *Sura 16:8* foretells modern modes of transportation. Again, the idea that Allah "creates what you don't know" in reference to modes of transportation isn't exactly a detailed and specific prophecy of *any* future event, much less a fulfilled prophecy predicting modern modes of transportation such as the jet airplane or the automobile.

Sura 30:41 foretells of "corruption" of the land and sea, a claim supporters say points to the pollution of the industrial age. Of course, corruption is a rather ambiguous term. Does it imply physical corruption, spiritual corruption, or some other form of corruption? This supposed prophecy is so vague, it can have a hundred different meanings to a hundred different people.

The Koran just didn't have what I was looking for. The types of prophecies I found in the Koran were imprecise and broad-based in nature. Nowhere could I find a prophecy that named a specific year, time, season, or place in which an event would occur. So I had to conclude that it lacked any sort of divine authority. But don't take my word for it. Read the Koran and find out for yourself.

Edgar Cayce

At the time of my research, another figure popularized in the media was Edgar Cayce. One of the most famous psychics in the history of the world, Cayce performed approximately 14,000 "readings" after falling into a self-induced state of sleep on his couch. For years, I encountered people who touted the great predictive powers of Edgar Cayce, but they never offered any specifics, just vague assertions. Curious, I decided to look into these readings for myself. After all, maybe Cayce really was a modern day prophet.

As luck would have it, the Edgar Cayce Association for Research and Enlightenment (C.A.R.E.) is located in Virginia Beach, not far from where I lived, so I was able to thoroughly investigate these claims in my own backyard, gathering information from the very foundation which is home to Cayce's life work.

Today, most of that work is available online. And according to the C.A.R.E. website, Cayce made a number of astounding predictions years in advance, such as predicting the 1929 stock market crash, World War II, and the Earth's polar shift.

For instance, it's claimed that in 1925, a young doctor received a reading from Cayce in which the psychic claimed he would soon come into a great windfall of wealth. After saying this, Cayce warned the doctor of "adverse forces that will come then in 1929" and to be very careful with his money *(Cayce Reading 2723-1)*. Of course, C.A.R.E. doesn't elaborate on whether or not the doctor ever received the wealth Cayce promised, but regardless – does "adverse forces in 1929" really qualify as a specific prediction of the 1929 stock market crash?

In another instance (six months before the 1929 crash),Cayce warned "we may expect a CONSIDERABLE break and bear market, see? This issue being between those of the reserves of nations and of INDIVIDUALS, and will cause – unless another of the more STABLE banking conditions come to the relief – a great disturbance in financial circles. This warning has been given, see?" (*Cayce Reading 900-425*).

This is more specific than the previous pronouncement, so it has greater credibility. But notice the key words here – "*may* expect…" and "*unless* another…" Charlatans often use such qualifiers so they can sidestep criticism if and when their predictions don't come true. If the stock market, *had not* crashed, then Cayce and his advocates could claim, "well, he said *maybe*…"

But the stock market did crash in 1929 leading to a "considerable bear market," right? Yes. It did. So for the sake of argument, let's say this Edgar Cayce prediction came true. Does that prove anything? Not really. After all, if you make over 14,000 predictions over the course of your life, some of them are bound to come true. Does that mean you have supernatural powers? Not necessarily.

And that's the case with Cayce as well. Over the course of his life, he made a number of predictions that didn't come true. For instance, in response to a person's question "What great change or the beginning of what change, if any, is to take place in the earth in the year 2,000 to 2,001 A.D.?" Cayce answered, "When there is a shifting of the poles; or a new cycle begins" (**Cayce Reading 826-8**).

Frankly, I'm not quite sure what that means, but the C.A.R.E. website claims it's a Cayce prediction of the earth's magnetic poles shifting sometime in 2000 or 2001. Either way, it didn't happen, so I don't see why so many people attribute great mystic, psychic, or prophetic powers to Edgar Cayce.

NOSTRADAMUS

For years, people I knew and many people in the popular media celebrated Nostradamus as a great prophet who predicted the future. So naturally I was curious, and I set out to examine his work for myself.

Born in 16th Century France, Nostradamus is most famous for his 1555 publication *The Prophecies*, a book which contains hundreds of verses.

In researching Nostradamus, I learned that his predictions were written in quatrains organized in several chapters known as 'Centuries.' Many people both then and now make bold claims concerning the prophetic significance of these writings, so it made sense to investigate them. His work is readily available on the Internet, so I encourage you to look up the verses that follow and draw your own conclusions.

One of Nostradamus's most famous quatrains, **Century II – Quatrain 24**, is heralded by proponents as proof positive of his grand insight into the future. They claim this passage foretells the rise of Adolph Hitler.

To those who believe in the prophetic significance of these verses, the key word is "Hister," which they immediately translate as "Hitler." However, "Hister" is the Latin name for the Danube River in Germany. Either way, it's clear to me that Nostradamus did not write the name "Hitler."

Even advocates of Nostradamus admit the original translation never directly names "Hitler." It's only through rearrangement of the letters in "Hister" that they come up with the name "Hitler." Of course, given the latitude to rearrange letters in a word, or add completely new letters, anyone's writings can be deemed "prophetic."

But maybe I'm not being fair to Nostradamus. So let's take a look at another Nostradamus prognostication, **Century I – Quatrain 60**. According to advocates, Nostradamus predicts the rise of Napoleon in this passage. If you haven't already, go look it up.

Clearly, it predicts the rise of Napoleon. Right? Yes, it does - as well as the rise of any historical person fitting this description, of which there are many. For example, Italian dictator Benito Mussolini was born in Italy, cost the empire dearly, and was more of a butcher than a prince.

When a newspaper horoscope states "You will see someone you know today," and then you see someone you know, this may in a technical sense qualify as a fulfilled prophecy. But would you ascribe supernatural inspiration to such an event? Of course you wouldn't. No rational person would. But that's exactly what has happened with the Nostradamus "prophecies."

Those vague and ambiguous quatrains which can be linked in some way to a modern event are heralded throughout the media as fulfilled prophecies, while the same pundits get a case of selective memory when it comes to the hundreds of additional quatrains which can't be linked to anything at all.

If you have any doubts concerning the legitimacy of the prophecies of Nostradamus, then I encourage you to find a full translation of his work and read it. Don't blindly accept my conclusions. Find out for yourself. Reading these quatrains firsthand, I believe you'll quickly conclude that the highly vaunted Nostradamus is nothing more than a media creation. Yet, inexplicably, there's no shortage of people willing to attribute prophetic power and supernatural significance to his writings.

If any doubts lingered as to the authority of Nostradamus as some sort of divine prophet, they should have been put to rest in July 1999. For in one of the rare quatrains where Nostradamus actually predicted a date [**Century X – Quatrain 72**], he failed miserably. Apparently, some sort of great king of terror should have appeared from the sky in July 1999. Yet July 1999 came and went, and no king of terror appeared from the sky. Maybe he came, and I just missed him. Nevertheless, I crossed Nostradamus off my list of credible sources long before July 1999.

MY CONCLUSION

Having personally investigated the claims of the world's great religious texts, philosophical writings, and secular prophets and psychics, I concluded that while elements of truth existed in many places throughout the world, most of the places championed by the world were flawed creations of men.

But I didn't view the Bible this way. Why? First, I believed the words of Jesus who constantly referenced the scriptures and called them "the power of God" (**Mark 12:24**), but I also had knowledge of the numerous specific prophecies in the Bible which were made far in advance of their fulfillment – prophecies I couldn't find anywhere else in the world. While I heard and investigated all the prophetic claims of Nostradamus and others, they didn't measure up to the astounding prophecies in the Bible. The Bible aced the test where all others failed.

It's the one book which contains verifiable evidence of divine authorship.

That's right. Evidence. Unlike other books, the Bible doesn't require blind acceptance or intellectual capitulation in order to believe in its divine origins. It offers concrete evidence.

So why is it that so many people think it doesn't? I think it's because most people haven't read the Bible and investigated it for themselves, and that's too bad.

Because the more I learned about fulfilled bible prophecy, the more I marveled at how I could remain ignorant of these prophecies for so long. Why weren't these prophecies common knowledge? Why weren't they taught in classrooms? How many people knew about them, and why didn't they tell me? And why wasn't the media trumpeting the Bible the way it trumpeted Nostradamus and Hollywood psychics?

These were questions I struggled to answer, because what I found in the Bible was nothing short of astounding. When objectively examined, I failed to see how anyone could conclude the Bible was anything less than what it claimed to be – the divine inspired Word of God. And I think when you examine for yourself the things that I found, you'll quickly draw the same conclusion.

CHAPTER 3
GOD'S FINGERPRINT

"Or let them tell us what the future holds, so we can know what's going to happen. Yes, tell us what will occur in the days ahead. Then we will know you are gods."

— Isaiah 41:22-23 (NLT)

I OFTEN HEAR PEOPLE say that if you believe the Bible is the Word of God, you're exhibiting "blind faith." Of course, the implication here is that if you believe the Bible, then you've abandoned all reason, because truly intelligent people think the Bible is a collection of ancient myths. But is this really true? Nope. I believe the Bible is the Word of God, and in doing so I haven't abandoned reason. In fact, it's just the opposite. Not believing the Bible is the Word of God is what requires the abandonment of reason – at least if you've taken the time to explore what's in the Bible. And most people haven't.

While faith is essential to a close relationship with God, "blind faith" implies there's no evidence for what you believe. This is a far cry from a true Christian faith.

The Bible defines faith as the certainty of what we hope for, but can't see (*Hebrews 11:1*). As Jesus told Thomas after he put his hands in the crucifixion wounds, "You believe because you have seen me. Blessed are those who believe without seeing me." ***John 20:29*** (NLT). In other words, faith is believing in the truth with certainty – even if you don't experience it first-hand. For instance, I believe Julius Caesar and Alexander the Great were real, historical human beings even though I've never seen either one of them, and I believe Julius Caesar crossed the Rubicon and became dictator of Rome even though I never saw him do it.

But in my opinion, it's much more reasonable to believe the Bible is the Word of God than to believe the historical accounts of Julius Caesar. Why? Well, first of all, I believe in Jesus, and I trust Him completely when He claims the Bible is the Word of God.

But that's my personal belief based on my faith in Jesus as a person and His personal credibility. For skeptics, "because Jesus said so" just doesn't cut it, and it shouldn't. But fulfilled prophecies made years in advance should.

Bible prophecy provides skeptics with clear evidence of the Bible's divine authority. No other book in the world can do this. No other book in the world can provide bona fide ***evidence*** of divine authorship. Only the Bible – of all the books in the history of the world – credibly predicts the future with 100% accuracy.

Keep in mind here that I'm not talking about daily newspaper horoscope-type predictions such as "you'll get out of bed today." I'm talking about detailed specific prophecies made hundreds and, in some cases, thousands of years in advance. Prophecies recorded by men from different time periods and life circumstances who claimed to be moved by God's Spirit. Yet despite their diversity in both time and circumstance, the words of those men fit together in perfect harmony. Why? Because none of these men prophesied on their own, they simply recorded God's Word as it was revealed to them (***2 Peter 1:20-21***).

The Bible is filled with historical examples of fulfilled prophecy. I'm going to cite a few examples in this chapter, but I'm not going to quote the actual verses, just reference them. Why? Because I want you to look up those verses for yourself. Don't just take my word for it. Investigate for yourself.

If you're too lazy to look up the verses, then you might as well put this book down right now. Some matters are just too important, and this is one of them. Don't blindly accept what I say or what anyone else says about the Bible. *That* would be "blind faith." Instead, when a Bible verse is referenced here, take the time to look it up. If you don't, you're not cheating me. You're only cheating yourself. Because God uses His Word to speak to us, and if you ignore Him, you'll miss what He's trying to tell you. What's He trying to tell you? That He's here. That He *does* exist, and that He's in complete control.

DANIEL AND ALEXANDER THE GREAT

More than six hundred years before Christ, and while exiled in Babylon, the prophet Daniel received a vision of a mighty goat who trampled a two-horned ram (*Daniel 8:5-7*). Soon after, the angel Gabriel appeared and explained the meaning of this vision. The ram represented the Media-Persian Empire and its two horns were the kings of Media and Persia, while the shaggy goat represented the Greek Empire and the goat's large horn represented the first king of the Greek Empire. The angel told Daniel that at the height of its power, the Greek Empire's king would die, and the Greek Empire would be broken into four kingdoms – none as great as the first (*Daniel 8:20-22*).

So did any of this happen? If you're familiar with history, you'll recognize that it did. In fact, all of it came true. In 334 B.C., Alexander the Great – the first king of the Greek Empire – began his invasion of the Media-Persian Empire, defeating Darius III and creating what was then the largest empire in the history of the world. Yet, in 323 B.C. at the height of his empire (just as Gabriel revealed), Alexander succumbed to a mysterious illness and died unexpectedly at age 33. Following his death, the Greek Empire broke into four kingdoms ruled by former generals in Alexander's army – Seleucus, Cassander, Ptolemy, and Lysimachus.

This is the same account catalogued in history books throughout the world – yet the Book of Daniel foretold these events more than 250 years before they transpired.

The Babylonian Empire Will Rule for 70 Years

Several years before Israel's exile in the land of Babylon, the prophet Jeremiah predicted that King Nebuchadnezzar would conquer Israel and Judah, carrying her people away as slaves. He also predicted Israel's exile in Babylon would end after 70 years of Babylonian rule over the nations (*Jeremiah 25:1-11*). History shows this is precisely what happened.

In 609 B.C., the Babylonians and the Medes defeated the armies of the Assyrian Empire at Harran, initiating the Babylonian Empire's rule over the nations of that region. In the decades that followed, King Nebuchadnezzar conquered the lands of Judah and Israel in a series of battles and carried her people to Babylon where they served as slaves. Then, in the year 539 B.C., Cyrus the Great conquered Babylon – ending the Babylonian Empire exactly 70 years after its rule began (609 B.C. – 539 B.C. = 70 years).

And the following year (538 B.C.), just as Jeremiah foretold, the Jewish captivity ended when Cyrus issued a decree allowing the Israelites to return to their homeland as part of his proclamation to rebuild Solomon's Temple.

Cyrus, King of Persia

Speaking of Cyrus and his proclamation – more than seven hundred years before Christ, the prophet Isaiah foretold the rise of a king named Cyrus who would give the command to rebuild Jerusalem and the Temple (*Isaiah 44:28*). He also described Cyrus as an instrument of the Lord who would leave great kings paralyzed with fear (*Isaiah 45:1*). Ultimately, God promised to use Cyrus to fulfill His purpose – to restore His city and free His captive people (*Isaiah 45:13*).

So did this happen? Yes – just as predicted. These prophecies were fulfilled to the letter approximately two hundred years later through the life of Cyrus the Great, King of Persia. In 539 B.C., Cyrus conquered Babylon, establishing the next great empire – the Media-Persian Empire. Then in 538 B.C., he issued a written proclamation to rebuild the Temple in Jerusalem, encouraging all the exiled people of Judah and Israel to return and participate in its rebuilding (*Ezra 1:1-8*).

ISRAEL'S DISPERSION AND EXILE

Years before it happened, the Bible predicted the worldwide dispersion and exile of the Jewish people. In the Book of Jeremiah, God said He would send war, famine, and disease upon the Israelites, scattering them throughout the world. Furthermore, He would make them an object of scorn and hatred in the exiled nations (*Jeremiah 29:17-19*).

In the Gospel of Luke, Jesus Himself declared that Jerusalem would soon be surrounded by armies and her people would be killed or sent away as captives in all the nations of the world (*Luke 21:23-24*).

So did all this happen as predicted? Yes. It happened just as the Bible said. In A.D. 70, the Roman legions led by Titus put an end to decades of Israeli insurrection, conquering its rebel armies and destroying the Jewish Temple. In an effort to eliminate Israel from the map and assimilate its people into the Empire, the Romans renamed the area Palestine and carted off its conquered citizens to the farthest edges of the Roman Empire to serve as slaves. Scattered among the nations of the world, the Jews faced widespread persecution and anti-Semitism. Thus the prophecies of both Jeremiah and Jesus were fulfilled.

But these are just a few examples. An exhaustive study of fulfilled bible prophecy is well beyond the scope of this book.

WERE THESE JUST HISTORICAL NOTATIONS?

But wait, you say. It's obvious what happened here. These aren't fulfilled prophecies at all – just historical accounts that you're reading after the fact and attributing to prophecy. After these historical events took place, the authors of the Old Testament wrote them down. Only later, did religious zealots like you call these recorded events "prophecies."

Believe that if you wish, but remember we've already covered the fact that I'm no religious zealot. I approach the Bible with the same open-mindedness with which I approach all other books. I want the truth. Just like you, I'm not looking for a fantasy to believe in.

If you attempt to explain away fulfilled bible prophecy as nothing more than back-dated history lessons, how do you account for the mountains of archaeological evidence showing that the Old Testament texts pre-date the historical events they chronicle?

But for the sake of argument, let's accept the idea that Old Testament prophecies are merely recorded history later misinterpreted as "prophecy". If this is really the case, then how do we explain away modern day fulfillment of bible prophecies from those same texts?

What's that? Did I just say *modern day* fulfillment of bible prophecy? Yes. You read that right. While the popular media is quick to discount the prophecies of the Bible while simultaneously glorifying Nostradamus, the modern world we live in is a prime witness to the predictive powers of the Bible. In fact, events from our own lifetime testify to the divine inspiration of the Bible as God's Holy Word.

THE MODERN NATION OF ISRAEL

Earlier we discussed the destruction of the Temple and the exile of the Jewish people following years of constant rebellion against their Roman oppressors. Tired of dealing with the troubles of the local people in this corner of their empire, the Romans set out to destroy every trace of the Jewish people. And in case you didn't know, the Roman people meant business. Just ask Carthage.

In the 3rd and 2nd Centuries B.C., Rome and Carthage fought three wars called the Punic wars. After more than one hundred years of fighting, Rome finally conquered Carthage (both the City and its empire), salting the earth so nothing would ever grow again. Their goal was to completely and utterly destroy Carthage as a nation and as a people. Did they succeed? I think so. Have you ever met a Carthaginian? I haven't either. But I've met quite a few Jews.

Despite the mighty Roman Empire's best efforts, the Jewish people miraculously retained their distinct racial, religious and cultural identity *for centuries* while living as exiles among the nations of the world. But how? Why do the Jewish people thrive to this day, while other ancient peoples have assimilated among the nations? Where are the Hittites, Ammonites, Edomites, Jebosites, and Philistines? The answer is found in the Bible.

The Jews are still around because of the God of Israel – the same God who promised Abraham his descendants would number more than the stars in the sky (*Genesis 15:5*). He's the same God who promised over and over again to bring His people out of exile and back into the land of Israel.

Does that promise sound familiar? It should.

Starting in the late 19th Century, thousands of Jews throughout the world started emigrating to the land of their ancestors. Decades of European anti-Semitism and Russian pogroms culminated in the Nazi Holocaust, convincing millions of Jews of a dire need to establish a Jewish state – not only as a means to escape persecution, but as a basic matter of survival. In 1948, this resulted in the modern state of Israel.

At the time, the rise of Israel surprised many world leaders. But it shouldn't have. Because God gave His Word through the Old Testament prophets that this is exactly what would happen.

THE RETURN OF GOD'S PEOPLE

The Bible not only predicted the dispersion and exile of the Jewish people among the nations, but it also predicted their return. The Old Testament is filled with God's promises to return His people home to Israel following a long, worldwide exile.

For instance, in *Isaiah 43:1-13* God comforts the Jewish people in exile, promising to bring them back to the land of Israel from east and west and north and south – from the farthest corners of the Earth. He also promises the Jewish people will survive and thrive despite the hardships they face in exile. In fact, God directly states the existence of the Jewish people in the land of Israel is evidence that He is the only God.

He challenges the nations of the world – can their idols foretell such things? Can any of them predict what will happen tomorrow? The implication, of course, is that they can't. But the God of Israel can! He fore-told of Israel's exile centuries in advance, and likewise, He proclaims their return. Now, skeptics will claim these prophecies are in reference to Israel's 70 year exile in Babylon – but clearly that's not the case. In Isaiah 43 and countless other verses, the Bible claims that God will call His people from "among the nations," from "the farthest corners of the earth," and "from north, south, east, and west" – not Babylon.

Almost everyone knows the story of Moses and God's deliverance of the Jewish people from Egyptian bondage. But thousands of years ago, the Bible predicted that a day would come when people no longer refer to the God of Israel as the one who rescued His people from the land of Egypt. Instead, they would refer to Him as the one who brought His people back into the land of Israel from ***all the countries in the world*** where He had exiled them (***Jeremiah 16:14-15***). That day has come.

In fact, whenever I think of the Jewish people, I think of the God of Abraham, Isaac, and Jacob who brought them into the modern day land of Israel.

Throughout the Old Testament, this is God's promise. He said… *I will bring "the remnant of my flock" back into the land of Israel* (***Jeremiah 23:3***). *I will bring them home from distant lands* (***Jeremiah 30:10***). *I will bring my people home and display my holiness to the nations* (***Ezekiel 20:41-42***). *I will bring you back from the lands where you are scattered* (***Ezekiel 20:34***).

In fact, God not only promised to bring His people back into the land, but into the very City of Jerusalem, saying – I will bring my people back from the countries where I have scattered them – to this very City (***Jeremiah 32:37***).

This happened following the end of the Six Day War in 1967. That war ended with Israel in control of Jerusalem for the first time in almost two millennia.

ISRAEL AS A SINGLE NATION

The prophet Isaiah promised that God would assemble the exiled people of Israel and form a new nation, raising its flag among the nations of the world (*Isaiah 11:12*). But he also predicted that when God's people returned, Israel and Judah would no longer be rivals, but the two would be united (*Isaiah 11:13*) – just as we see today with the modern state of Israel.

The prophet Ezekiel also made this proclamation, stating that Israel would be one kingdom, no longer divided (*Ezekiel 37:22*). Since its establishment in May 1948, the state of Israel has remained politically united as one nation state with a single, unified government.

ISRAEL'S THRIVING AGRICULTURE

Also in the Book of Isaiah, God promised to not only bring Jacob's descendants (the Jewish people) back into the land of Israel, but He also promised that Israel would blossom agriculturally and fill the whole world with its fruit (*Isaiah 27:6*). Today, the tiny nation of Israel (a desert wasteland less than a century ago) is one of the world's leading fresh citrus producers and a net exporter of more than forty varieties of fruit.

ISRAEL CREATED IN A SINGLE DAY

More than 2,500 years before it happened, the prophet Isaiah predicted that God would bring forth the nation of Israel in a single day. He likened it to a woman "who gives birth in an instant without labor pains" (*Isaiah 66:7-9*).

On 14 May 1948 (the day when the British Mandate over Palestine expired), the Jewish People's Council met at the Tel Aviv Museum and approved a proclamation declaring the establishment of the state of Israel. The United States formally recognized the Jewish state **on that same day**. And a new nation had come into being in a single day, just as the prophet Isaiah foretold.

DISPUTES OVER THE LAND

Seven hundred years before Christ, the prophet Ezekiel foretold of a day when the inhabitants of Jerusalem would say about the Jewish exiles, "They are far from God, so He has given their land to us." But God promised to safeguard His exiled people and bring them back to their land once again (*Ezekiel 11:14-17*).

In another passage, God again promised to gather His people once again in the land of Israel where they will live safely, plant vineyards, and build homes. But the neighboring nations who treat these returned exiles with contempt will be punished (*Ezekiel 28:25-26*).

Since its inception in May 1948, the modern state of Israel has engaged in no less than a half dozen wars with the nations around her. And why? Because her neighbors claim the land belongs to them – just as Ezekiel prophesied more than 2,600 years ago.

THE VALLEY OF DRY BONES

Hundreds of years before Titus and the Roman legions destroyed the Temple and initiated the Jewish exile among the nations, the prophet Ezekiel received a vision from God. Ezekiel prophesied, then dry bones in a valley started piecing themselves together into skeleton form, then muscle, flesh, and skin appeared. But the bones had no life until God breathed life into them (*Ezekiel 37:7-10*).

God explained this vision in clear terms. The bones represented the exiled people of Israel. God promised that when they are saying, "our hope is gone" and "our nation is dead," He would open their graves and bring them back into the land of Israel (*Ezekiel 37:11-14*).

The Jewish people were saying exactly these things in the aftermath of the Holocaust. The Nazi "Final Solution" killed six million Jews, and had the war not ended when it did, it's likely that all the Jews in Europe would have perished. But out of this abyss of evil and despair, God breathed new life into the Jewish people – bringing them back into the land of Israel just as He had promised.

NEVER AGAIN TO BE UPROOTED

While many of Israel's neighbors would love to see the Jewish state destroyed, what they fail to realize is that God has promised they will never leave. According to the Book of Amos, God promised to bring His people back from the faraway lands where they were exiled and firmly plant His people in Israel, never to be uprooted again (*Amos 9:11-15*). Given the impeccable track record of bible prophecy, this should be a clear message to Israel's enemies. Despite Mahmoud Ahmadinejad's promise to "wipe Israel off the map," God has other plans. Would you bet against Him?

PUTTING IT ALL IN PERSPECTIVE

The Old Testament prophets recorded these pronouncements from God more 600 years before Christ – hundreds of years before Roman conquerors exiled the Jewish people from the land of Israel and more than 2,000 years before they returned and established the modern state of Israel. In spite of skeptics who say the Bible is just mythology, the Jewish people returned to Israel and re-established their nation – just as God said they would after almost 1,900 years of exile among the nations. Still think belief in the Bible requires "blind faith"? Or is it really the other way around?

CONCLUSION

So what should you conclude from reading all these fulfilled prophecies? That's for you to decide. But as for me – uncovering fulfilled bible prophecy helped me find many of the answers I had once sought. I now knew… *There is a God, and He really does exist.*

I also knew who He was… *He's the God of Israel. The God of Abraham, Isaac, and Jacob.*

Furthermore, I now believed… *The Bible is the Word of God.*

The modern state of Israel and the continued survival of the Jewish people who live there testify to the very existence of God. The Bible stands apart from all other texts in its unparalleled track record of fulfilled prophecies made hundreds (and sometimes thousands) of years in advance. No other book, psychic, or soothsayer even approaches the track record of the Bible when it comes to fulfilled prophecies. Those who contend the Bible is just a collection of ancient stories written by regular Joe's need to explain its fulfilled prophecies. Outside of a supernatural explanation, I don't see how they can.

The truth is these prophecies serve a specific purpose. They not only reveal the existence of an all-knowing Creator, they push us toward a closer relationship with Him.

In bible prophecy, I found what I was searching for. Evidence of divine authority. In the Bible, I found a credible starting point in my search for truth, one that opened the door for a whole host of exciting revelations which would transform my life for the better.

Why? Because not only did the Bible predict historical events involving ancient empires and the modern state of Israel, it also contained a subset of prophecies concerning the coming of a Messiah born to be the Savior of the world. And you want to know the best part? He wants *you* to be His close personal friend. Not only does He want it, He yearns for it! Believe it or not, God loves *you*.

So who is this Messiah? You probably hear His name every day as you go about your daily routine. I know I do, and His name is regularly spoken by a whole host of people – even those who ***don't*** believe in Him. He literally conquered death out of a love for you, and He's been clamoring to get your attention for years. How? Any number of ways, which include (but are certainly not limited to) giving sight to the blind, opening the ears of the deaf, and healing lepers and quadriplegics. Oh yeah, and He also brought some dead people back to life.

Did any of that get your attention? If not, I'm sure He's open to recommendations – after all, despite the fact that He's Lord of the Universe, He's quite approachable. In fact, if you don't already know Him, He's begging you to acknowledge Him and talk to Him right now. Why would He want to talk to you? As I've already said, He wants to be friends with *you*.

CHAPTER 4

CHAPTER 4
THE MESSIANIC PROPHECIES

"For a child is born to us, a son is given to us. The government will rest on his shoulders. And he will be called: Wonderful Counselor, Mighty God, Everlasting Father, Prince of Peace."

— Isaiah 9:6 (NLT)

A POPULAR SONG BACK in the mid-90's was Joan Osbourne's *What If God Was One Of Us?* The song asks you to imagine what it would be like if God became one of us, just like a regular stranger you saw on the bus. Seems like an interesting thought, huh? After all, what would God's name be? What would His face look like? To most people, the idea that this could happen seems a little far-fetched.

But this isn't something we have to imagine. God ***did*** become one of us. He became a man in the flesh and walked among us.

Throughout my life, I've heard countless people say, "If God really exists, then why doesn't He reveal Himself?" The simple fact of the matter is that He has! The problem is most people either don't accept that He has, remain ignorant of the facts surrounding His arrival, or they just plain aren't paying attention. Are you one of them? I once was. At the time, you could've labeled me as both "ignorant" and "not paying attention." Yet God was all around me. In fact, the Bible says creation itself is screaming out in testimony of His existence (**Romans 1:20**).

One of the reasons people ask, "Where is God?" is because they would expect an Almighty powerful God to show Himself to us high up in the sky with a loud booming voice, thunder, lightning, and billowing smoke – loudly proclaiming His presence. "I AM!" He would say. Why do people think this? Because this is how most people would announce themselves if they were the all-powerful God of the universe. Come on now, don't pretend otherwise. That's exactly what you would do, right? So why doesn't the real God of the Universe do this?

Believe it or not, He **did**. God appeared in this very form to the Israelites on Mount Sinai, but they were overcome with fear and told Moses, "Don't let God speak to us like this or we'll die!" (**Exodus 20:18-19**). The Israelites were frightened out of their minds! Wouldn't you be if you heard thunder and lightning and a booming voice from heaven?

So God honored the request of the Israelites to no longer speak to people this way. Instead, He promised to raise up a prophet from among the Israelites. God would tell the people everything He needed to tell them by putting His own words in the mouth of this prophet (**Deuteronomy 18:15-18**).

So who is this prophet promised by God? He's known as the Messiah, and the Old Testament is filled with countless prophecies describing Him. Just as God foretold the rise and fall of world empires when He revealed Nebuchadnezzar's dream and its meaning to Daniel (**Daniel 2:27**), He also foretold the coming of a Messiah who would be Savior of the world. In fact, the New Testament tells us that the Word of God, which was God and through which all things were created, became flesh and dwelled among us (**John 1:14**).

So if God **was** one of us as Joan Osbourne so eloquently put it, then what was His name? It's a name you've probably heard throughout your life. His name was Jesus – Jesus of Nazareth. Some call Him Jesus Christ – with Christ being the Greek word for Messiah. Yes, God entered the form of a human and revealed Himself to the world through Jesus Christ.

Now, if you don't already believe in Jesus, you might be a bit skeptical, and I can't blame you. After all, most religions and cults throughout history have worshiped "man-gods." Even government officials such as the Egyptian pharaohs and the Roman Caesars were once worshipped as gods.

Modern day cults often worship their leaders as well. Jim Jones, Marshall Applewhite, and David Koresh are a few recent examples. Most of their followers ended up dead, and it's obvious to the rest of us those men were fakes – false Messiahs. So what makes Jesus any different?

A number of things make Jesus stand apart from these other historical figures, and one that should really make you pause if you're a skeptic is bible prophecy. Why? Because the same Bible which prophesied the rise and fall of world empires and the re-establishment of Israel as a nation with 100% accuracy, is the same Bible which prophesied the coming of a Jewish Messiah who would offer His life as a sacrifice for the sins of the world.

And every prophecy the Bible made about this Messiah came true in the life of one man, and one man only – Jesus of Nazareth. So maybe you should give Jesus a chance. After all, how many people can claim that on their resume?

THE MESSIANIC PROPHECIES

I believe that a careful examination of the Old Testament Messianic prophecies reveals that Jesus of Nazareth fulfilled *all of them*. But again, don't take my word for it. Do some research and read them for yourself. Here are just a few examples.

1) **Born in Bethlehem** – Approximately 700 years before the birth of Jesus, the prophet Micah predicted the Messiah would be born in Bethlehem. He claimed that while Bethlehem is only a small village in Judah, a ruler of Israel whose origins are from the distant past will come from Bethlehem (*Micah 5:2*).

    Was Jesus born in Bethlehem? Yes. Shortly before His birth, the Roman Emperor decreed a census be taken throughout the Empire. As part of the census, people were required to return to their ancestral towns to register. As a descendant of King David, Joseph was required to go to Bethlehem, taking his wife Mary with him (*Luke 2:1-5*). And while they were there, Jesus was born in Bethlehem (*Matthew 2:1*).

2) **Born of a Virgin** – 2,700 years ago, the prophet Isaiah relayed a message from God to King Ahaz. In His message, God promised to send a sign. What kind of sign? A virgin would give birth to a child and name Him Immanuel, which means "God is with us" (*Isaiah 7:14*).

Jesus fulfilled this prophecy as well. His mother, Mary, was engaged to be married to Joseph. But while she was still engaged, she became pregnant through the power of the Holy Spirit. Joseph considered breaking the engagement, until an angel appeared to him in a dream and confirmed that the child was conceived of the Holy Spirit. The angel said to name Him Jesus because He would save people from their sins (*Matthew 1:18-21*).

3) **A Descendant of Judah** – In his last words to his sons nearly 4,000 years ago, Jacob revealed that the ruling scepter would not depart from Judah, noting that the Messiah (the one who all nations will serve) will be from the family of Judah (*Genesis 49:10*).

The Gospels confirm that Jesus was descended from Judah (*Luke 3:23-38, Matthew 1:1-17*).

4) **Great Kings Will Pay Homage and Tribute** – Three thousand years ago, Solomon predicted the Western kings of Tarshish and the eastern kings of Sheba and Seba would bestow gifts upon the Messiah (*Psalm 72:10*).

This happened to Jesus as well. After He was born, some wise men from eastern lands followed a star in the sky to Bethlehem. When they arrived and saw Mary and Jesus, they bowed down to worship Him, opening their treasure chests and giving Him gifts of gold, frankincense, and myrrh (*Matthew 2:1-2,11*).

5) **A Descendant of David** – More than a thousand years before Jesus was born, God promised David He would place one of his descendants on the throne, and the royal line of David would continue forever and ever (*Psalm 132:11-12*). Three hundred years after David, the prophet Jeremiah revealed that God would raise up a righteous descendant who rules with wisdom from the line of King David (*Jeremiah 23:5-6, 33:15*).

So was Jesus a descendant of King David? Yes. When the angel Gabriel appeared to Mary and informed her that she would give birth to a son, he revealed that Jesus would called the Son of the Most High, and God would give Him the throne of His ancestor David (*Luke 1:32-33*). The Gospel of Matthew also provides a family lineage of Jesus which traces His roots back to King David (*Matthew 1:1-17*).

6) **Taken to Egypt** – 2,700 years ago, the prophet Hosea predicted that the Messiah would be called out of Egypt (*Hosea 11:1*).

Was Jesus called out of Egypt? Yes. After Jesus' birth, an angel appeared to Joseph and told him to flee to Egypt because King Herod was trying to kill the newborn child. So Joseph, Mary, and Jesus fled to Egypt. When Herod died, an angel of God appeared in Joseph's dream and told him it was safe to take Mary and Jesus back to Israel (*Matthew 2:13-20*).

7) **Heralded by a Messenger** – 2,700 years ago, the prophet Isaiah revealed that the arrival of the Messiah would be preceded by a messenger – a voice crying in the wilderness, "Make a straight pathway for our God!" This messenger would shout from the mountaintops, telling Jerusalem and the towns of Judah, "Your God is coming!" (*Isaiah 40:3-11*).

So did such a messenger precede Jesus? Yes. Before Jesus began His ministry, the Jewish leaders sent a group of men to ask John the Baptist who he was. When John said he was not the Messiah, they asked, "Then who are you?" John echoed these very words written by Isaiah, stating

"I am a voice shouting in the wilderness. Clear a straight path for the Lord!" (*John 1:19-27*). This is the same John the Baptist who testified that Jesus was the Lamb of God who takes away the sin of the world.

8) **Is the Son of God** – God promised to proclaim to the Messiah "you are my son, and today I have become your Father" (*Psalm 2:7-8*).

This happened to Jesus as well. After being baptized by John, Jesus came out of the water, the heavens opened up, and God's Spirit descended upon Him like a dove. A voice from heaven then said, "This is my son in whom I am well pleased" (*Matthew 3:17*).

9) **Anointed by the Holy Spirit** – Isaiah also prophesied that out of the stump of David, a shoot will grow, and the Spirit of the Lord will rest upon Him (*Isaiah 11:2*). This is a prophecy stating that God's Spirit will come to rest upon the Messiah.

Did anything like this happen to Jesus? Yes. Following His baptism, the heavens opened up and the Spirit of God descended like a dove and came to rest upon Jesus (*Matthew 3:16-17*).

10) **Brings Light to Galilee** – 2,700 years ago, Isaiah prophesied that there would come a time in the future when Galilee of the Gentiles which lies between the Jordan and the sea would be filled with glory. A light would shine for the people who walk in darkness, for a child will be born and His name will be Wonderful Counselor, Mighty God, Everlasting Father, and Prince of Peace (*Isaiah 9:1-7*). In other words, the Messiah would first appear in Galilee.

So did Jesus first appear in Galilee? Yes. The Town of Nazareth was located in the province of Galilee between the Jordan River and the Mediterranean Sea. Raised in Nazareth, Jesus began His ministry in Galilee, preaching first in Nazareth and then in Capernaum (*Matthew 4:12-17*).

11) **The Sick Will Be Healed** – Seven hundred years before Jesus began His ministry, Isaiah prophesied that God would come to save His people, and when He comes, He will heal the blind, the deaf, the

lame, and the mute (*Isaiah 35:5-6*). Later, Isaiah says the Messiah will be weighed down by our sicknesses and diseases (*Isaiah 53:4*). So according to Isaiah, the Messiah would heal the sick.

So did Jesus do this? On many occasions. In one such instance, Jesus healed a man with leprosy (*Matthew 8:1-4*). On other occasions, He healed a man with a deformed hand (*Matthew 12:9-14*). He cured Simon Peter's mother-in-law of her fever and healed many people who were sick with varying diseases (*Mark 1:29-34*). He healed a woman who suffered bleeding for 12 years (*Mark 5:24-34*). He cured a woman who had been crippled for 18 years (*Luke 13:10-17*). He healed ten lepers simultaneously (*Luke 17:11-19*), and He healed the dying son of a government official from Capernaum (*John 4:46-54*). And there are many other instances where Jesus healed the sick.

12) **The Blind Will See** – Isaiah also prophesied that the Messiah would be a light unto the nations and would open the eyes of the blind (*Isaiah 42:6-7*).

So did Jesus open the eyes of the blind? Yes. The Gospels testify to numerous instances where Jesus healed the blind. For instance, Jesus healed a blind beggar named Bartimaeus (*Mark 10:46-52*). He also healed two blind men (*Matthew 9:27-31*), and He cured another blind man by spitting on the ground, rubbing mud in the man's eyes, and having him wash the mud off in the pool of Siloam (*John 9:1-12*).

13) **The Deaf Will Hear** – Isaiah also prophesied that when the Messiah comes, the deaf will hear (*Isaiah 29:18-19*), for the Messiah will unplug the ears of the deaf (*Isaiah 35:5*).

So did Jesus restore hearing to the deaf? Yes. In one such instance, Jesus put His fingers in the ears of a deaf man with a speech impediment, touched the man's tongue, and said "be opened!" and the man could hear (*Mark 7:31-37*). Another time, a demon-possessed boy was unable to hear or speak. Jesus rebuked the demon, and it left the boy (*Mark 9:14-29*).

14) The Lame Will Walk – Isaiah also prophesied that the Messiah would have power to cure the paralyzed, that the lame will leap like a deer (*Isaiah 35:5-6*).

Did Jesus heal the paralyzed? Yes. When some people brought a paralyzed man on a mat to Jesus, He told the man, "Your sins are forgiven. Stand up, pick up your mat, and go home!" Instantly, the man hopped up and went home (*Matthew 9:1-8*). While in Jerusalem, Jesus saw a man who had been paralyzed for 38 years. He told the man, "Stand up, pick up your mat, and walk!" and in an instant, the man was healed (*John 5:1-18*).

15) Will Raise The Dead – 2,500 years ago, the prophet Zechariah revealed that the Messiah would resurrect the dead (*Zechariah 9:11*).

Did Jesus do this? Yes. He not only raised Himself from the dead, but the Gospels also record several instances where He raised others from the dead. For instance, Jairus' 12 year-old daughter was pronounced dead, but when Jesus entered her home, took hold of her hand, and said "Little girl, get up," she immediately stood up and started walking around (*Mark 5:21-43*). Outside the village of Nain, Jesus encountered a funeral procession for a widow's only son. He approached the coffin and told the boy, "get up!" And the dead boy sat up and talked (*Luke 7:11-17*). Although Lazarus had been dead in his grave for four days, Jesus ordered his tomb opened and said, "Lazarus, come out!" And Lazarus walked out of his tomb (*John 11:1-44*).

16) Enters Jerusalem on a Donkey – 2,500 years ago, the prophet Zechariah said the Messiah will ride into Jerusalem to shouts of triumph, and while He is all-powerful, He will humble Himself by riding on a donkey's colt (*Zechariah 9:9*).

So did Jesus ride into Jerusalem on a donkey to shouts of triumph? Yes. Five hundred years after Zechariah's prophecy, Jesus rode into Jerusalem on a donkey's colt. The crowds spread their clothes and palm branches on the ground before Him, singing praises to God for the one who comes in the name of the Lord (*Matthew 21:1-11*).

17) **He Will Enter the Temple** – Approximately 500 years before the birth of Christ, God proclaimed through the prophet Malachi that He would send a messenger ahead of Himself to prepare the way, and then the Lord everyone is seeking will come to His Temple (*Malachi 3:1*). In other words, the Messiah would be preceded by a messenger and then enter His Temple.

Jesus was preceded by a messenger (John the Baptist), and then He entered the Temple where He overturned the tables of the money changers (*John 2:13-22*). Keep in mind that the Romans destroyed the Temple almost 2,000 years ago, so no one who has lived since then is capable of fulfilling this prophecy.

18) **Betrayed by a Friend** – Over 3,000 years ago, King David prophesied that the Messiah would be betrayed by a trusted best friend, a person so close they shared each other's food (*Psalm 41:9*).

Did this happen to Jesus? Yes. A thousand years later, David's prophecy was fulfilled when Jesus predicted His betrayal at the last supper. He told the disciples He would dip His bread in a bowl and hand it to the one who would betray Him. He did so and handed the bread to Judas (*John 13:21-30*). Judas then left the room and went off to betray Jesus.

19) **Betrayed for 30 Pieces of Silver** – Five hundred years before it happened, the prophet Zechariah foretold the exact price for which the Messiah would be betrayed – 30 pieces of silver (*Zechariah 11:12*).

After Jesus dipped His bread in the bowl and handed it to Judas, Judas went to the Jewish priests and elders and betrayed Jesus for the exact sum of 30 pieces of silver (*Matthew 26:14-15*).

20) **Thrown into the Potter's Field** – Five hundred years before Judas betrayed Jesus, God told the prophet Zechariah that the 30 pieces of

silver, the great sum at which He was valued, would be thrown in the potter's field (*Zechariah 11:13*).

So what is a potter's field? In ancient times, the potter's field was the place of burial for unknown or indigent people. Clay was extracted from the fields for the production of pottery, but the leftover field was only useful as a burial ground.

When Judas betrayed Jesus to the Jewish priests and elders, they paid him 30 pieces of silver. But when he realized what he had done, Judas returned and tried to give the money back. When they wouldn't take it, he threw the money down in the Temple. Thinking it not right to put blood money in the Temple treasury, the leading priests used the money to buy a potter's field for the burial of foreigners (*Matthew 27:3-8*).

21) **Will Be Rejected** – 2,700 years ago, the prophet Isaiah described the Messiah as "despised and rejected," a man familiar with the deepest sadness. The people would turn their backs on Him (*Isaiah 53:3*).

When Jesus was brought before Pilate, Pilate presented Him to the people and said, "Here is your king." But the people demanded He be crucified. "Crucify your king?" Pilate responded. But the people said, "We have no king but Caesar" (*John 19:14-15*). Jesus was rejected as king and despised by the leaders of His day, yet as Peter said, "the stone rejected by the builders has become the cornerstone" thus fulfilling Psalm 118:22 (*Acts 4:11*).

22) **Silent in Front of His Accusers** – Seven hundred years before Jesus was brought before the High Council and accused of blasphemy, the prophet Isaiah claimed the Messiah would be silent when faced by His accusers, much like a sheep is silent before the shearers (*Isaiah 53:7*).

Was Jesus silent before His accusers? He was. When the high priest Caiaphas asked Jesus, "What do you have to say for yourself? How do you answer these charges?" Jesus was silent (*Matthew 26:62-63*).

23) **Accused by False Witnesses** – A thousand years earlier, King David predicted the Messiah would be accused and slandered by false witnesses (*Psalm 35:11*). He prophesied these false witnesses would claim, "We saw Him do it with our own eyes" (*Psalm 35:21*).

Is this what happened to Jesus? Yes. The leading priests and the high council couldn't find any evidence against Jesus. So many false witnesses testified against Him saying, "We ourselves heard Him say, 'I will destroy this Temple made with human hands and raise another in three days made without human hands.'" But even the lying witnesses couldn't get their stories straight (*Mark 14:55-59*).

24) **Will Be Beaten, Mocked, and Spit Upon** – More than 700 years before the crucifixion, the prophet Isaiah said the Messiah would give His back to those who beat Him, His cheeks to those who pull His beard, and His face to those who mock and spit upon Him (*Isaiah 50:6*).

Does this describe Jesus? Yes. After Caiaphas tore his own clothing and accused Jesus of blasphemy, the other accusers shouted "Guilty!" They spit in Jesus' face and beat Him with their fist. Then, they mocked Him, saying "prophesy to us Messiah – who hit you that time?" (*Matthew 26:67*).

25) **Will Be Beaten, Bloodied, and Disfigured** – Centuries before the crucifixion, the prophet Isaiah said the Messiah's face would be so disfigured few would hardly recognize Him as human (*Isaiah 52:13-14*).

Is this the case with Jesus? Yes. Before the crucifixion, Pilate had Jesus flogged with a lead-tipped whip, and the Roman soldiers fit a crown of thorns upon His head (*John 19:1-3*). This would have severely disfigured Jesus.

26) **Will Be Mocked and Told to Save Himself** – A thousand years before the cross, King David prophesied the Messiah would be mocked by

onlookers who will say, "The Lord loves Him so much, huh? Let the Lord save Him now" (*Psalm 22:7-8*).

This is precisely what happened to Jesus. While He was being crucified, the people mocked Jesus saying, "Save yourself and come down from the cross." The religious leaders also mocked Jesus saying, "He saved others, but He can't save Himself. If He's the King of Israel, let Him come down from that cross and then we'll believe. If He's the Son of God, let God save Him now" (*Matthew 27:39-44*).

27) **Pierced Hands and Feet** – A thousand years before Jesus was crucified, King David prophesied that the Messiah's hands and feet would be pierced (*Psalm 22:16*).

Were Jesus' hands and feet pierced? Yes. Forced to carry His own cross, Jesus was taken to a place called Golgotha, where He was nailed to the cross. Two others were crucified also, one on either side of Him (*John 19:17-18*). The very method of crucifixion required the Roman soldiers to drive nails through Jesus' hands and feet. Even though crucifixion wasn't invented at the time of King David's prophecy (in those days the preferred method of execution was stoning), every letter of this prophecy was fulfilled when Jesus was crucified.

28) **Will Be Given Vinegar and Gall to Drink** – A thousand years before the crucifixion, King David predicted the Messiah would be given gall (poison) for food and sour wine to quench His thirst (*Psalm 69:21*).

Did this happen to Jesus? Yes. When they arrived at Golgotha, the soldiers gave Jesus wine mixed with bitter gall (poison), but when He tasted it, He refused to drink it (*Matthew 27:34*). One of the bystanders at the crucifixion filled a sponge with sour wine and held it up to Jesus on a stick so He could drink it (*Mark 15:36*).

29) **His Clothes Divided Up** – A thousand years before the crucifixion, King David prophesied that others would cast lots to determine who would get the Messiah's garments at His execution (*Psalm 22:17-18*).

Did this happen to Jesus? Yes. When the Roman soldiers crucified

Jesus, they divided His clothes among themselves. But His robe was a single garment, woven from top to bottom, and they didn't want to tear it. So rather than tear it, they decided to throw dice to see who got it (*John 19:23-24*).

30) **His Bones Not Broken** – King David also prophesied that the bones of a righteous person would never be broken (*Psalm 34:19-20*). Only one righteous person ever lived – the Messiah, Jesus Christ. And His bones were never broken, despite His being crucified!

The day of the crucifixion was also the day of preparation (the next day was Passover), and the Jewish leaders didn't want the crucified bodies hanging in public on a Sabbath. So they asked Pilate to speed up the executions by breaking the legs of those who were being crucified. Pilate agreed and the soldiers broke the legs of the two men being crucified with Jesus, but when the soldiers got to Jesus, they did not break His legs, because they saw that He was already dead (*John 19:31-33*).

31) **The Messiah's Side Will Be Pierced** – Five hundred years before the crucifixion, Zechariah prophesied that the people of Israel will look upon me (the Messiah) whom they have pierced and mourn for Him as for an only son (*Zechariah 12:10*).

Was Jesus pierced? Yes. One of the Roman soldiers pierced Jesus with a spear (*John 19:34*).

32) **Life Poured Out Like Water** – In a psalm which depicts a detailed description of death by crucifixion (even though this method of execution hadn't been invented yet), King David prophesied that the Messiah's life would be poured out like water (*Psalm 22:14*).

So is this what happened to Jesus? Yes. When the soldiers went to break Jesus' legs, and they saw He was already dead, one of the soldiers pierced the side of Jesus and blood and water flowed out (*John 19:34*).

33) **Will Be Struck Down and His Disciples Scattered** – Five hundred years before Jesus, the prophet Zechariah prophesied that the Messiah

would be struck down, and His followers scattered, declaring, "Strike down the shepherd, and His sheep will be scattered" (*Zechariah 13:7*).

At the last supper, Jesus (quoting *Zechariah 13:7*) told His disciples that they would desert Him on that very night (*Matthew 26:31*). That night, when Jesus was betrayed and arrested in Gethsemane, all the disciples deserted Him and fled (*Matthew 26:56*).

34) **Will Be Buried in a Rich Man's Grave** – Hundreds of years before Jesus' execution, the prophet Isaiah predicted that the Messiah would be treated like a common criminal and buried in a rich man's tomb (*Isaiah 53:9*).

Did this happen to Jesus? Yes. As evening approached on the day of the crucifixion, a rich man named Joseph of Arimathea (one of Jesus' followers) asked Pilate for Jesus' body. Pilate agreed to release the body, and Joseph wrapped it in a clean sheet of linen cloth. Then he placed Jesus' body in the tomb he had prepared for himself, sealing it by rolling a boulder into the entrance (*Matthew 27:59-60*).

35) **Will Rise from the Dead** – A thousand years before the resurrection, King David prophesied that the Messiah's body would not be left among the dead, that God would not allow His Holy One to rot in the grave (*Psalm 16:10*). Psalm 49 reveals that God will restore the Messiah's life, saving Him from the power of the grave (*Psalm 49:15*).

Three days and three nights after the crucifixion, Mary and Mary Magdalene went to visit the tomb. When they arrived, a great earthquake shook the ground. The angel of the Lord came down from heaven, the rock rolled away from the tomb's entrance, the Roman soldiers guarding the tomb fainted, and the angel spoke to the two women, telling them Jesus had risen from the dead just as He had promised (*Matthew 28:5-7*).

36) **Will Ascend to Heaven** – A thousand years before the resurrection, King David prophesied that the Messiah would ascend to heaven (*Psalm 68:18*).

Did Jesus ascend to heaven? Yes. According to the Gospel of Luke,

Jesus was taken up to heaven while blessing the disciples (*Luke 24:51*). The Book of Acts says that after talking to the disciples, Jesus was lifted up into a white cloud, and the disciples strained to see Him as He ascended into heaven (*Acts 1:9-11*).

37) **Will Be Served by Future Generations** – King David also prophesied that the Messiah would be served by our children, and future generations will hear about His wonders (*Psalm 22:30*).

Have future generations heard about the wonders of Jesus? You bet. Every generation since the crucifixion of Christ has heard of his righteous acts and everything He has done. Today, consciously or unconsciously, the name of Jesus graces the lips of everyone on the face of the earth.

SO WHAT DOES THIS MEAN?

That's all well and good you might say, but you're heavily reliant on the New Testament to verify that Jesus fulfilled these prophecies. How can we be sure the New Testament is reliable? This is where faith comes into play – not a faith built on blind acceptance, but a faith built on trust.

Remember, the same Bible predicted the gathering of the Jews from the farthest corners of the earth to re-establish the nation of Israel. That's something you can see today with your own eyes. And the same Bible predicted the Medes would conquer Babylon and the Greek Empire would break up into four kingdoms.

But again, don't take my word for it, many historians and archeologists will vouch for the credibility of the New Testament as an accurate historical account. Making that case, though, is far beyond the scope of this book. So I encourage you to examine these claims for yourself. A good place to start is *The Case for Christ* by Lee Strobel.

CONCLUSION

Only one person fulfilled the Old Testament Messianic prophecies with 100% accuracy – Jesus of Nazareth. No one else. Now if you're a skeptic, you might say He set out to fulfill these prophecies, and He and His disciples made up stories and arranged His life so He could claim fulfillment of these prophecies. But if that's the case, how did they arrange the town in which He was born? Or who His descendants were? Or the price paid for His betrayal? They couldn't.

While Jesus and His disciples could certainly arrange the fulfillment of *some* of the prophecies (such as riding into Jerusalem on a donkey), they certainly couldn't dictate the circumstances and the timing of them all. For instance, if you're a fraud, how do you arrange the healing of a blind man or raise someone from the dead?

The fact of the matter is that it's highly unlikely *anyone* would fulfill all of these prophecies, yet Jesus did. How unlikely? Let's say you had a 50/50 chance of fulfilling each of the prophecies just noted. Your odds of success are two to the 37th power – or 1 in 137,438,953,472. So with just a 1 in 2 chance of fulfilling each prophecy, only one out of every 137 billion people would be successful! And that's assuming your odds are 50/50. Do you really think the average person has a 50/50 chance of being born in Bethlehem? Of being buried in a rich man's tomb or even entering a Temple that was destroyed almost 2,000 years ago?

Probably not.

But even so, the odds are still greater than 1 in 137 billion. Why? Because the Old Testament predicted the time of the Messiah's arrival, and that time has long since passed. Because of that, no one born since that time or who is born in the future can ever fully fulfill the Messianic prophecies. Only one man could and only one man did, and the *exact* time of His arrival was foretold by Daniel more than 2,600 years ago.

CHAPTER 5
THE TIME OF HIS COMING

"One day the Pharisees and Sadducees came to test Jesus, demanding that he show them a miraculous sign from heaven to prove his authority. He replied, "You know the saying, 'Red sky at night means fair weather tomorrow; red sky in the morning means foul weather all day.' You know how to interpret the weather signs in the sky, but you don't know how to interpret the signs of the times!"

— Matthew 16:1-3 (NLT)

SO WHAT DID Jesus mean when He referred to the "signs of the times"? What signs? And what times?

Many people believe Jesus was pointing to the miracles He had already performed as evidence of who He was, and this is partially true. Much like the traditional expression "where there's smoke, there's fire," Jesus was basically saying that enough evidence of who He was had already been presented.

First, let's remember who the Pharisees and Sadducees were. They were self-proclaimed scriptural experts, and as a group they ***did*** know the scriptures well – at least in letter if not in spirit. This means they had full knowledge of the Messianic prophecies, and they knew exactly what to "look" for when the Messiah appeared, much in the same way that you and I can look at a dark, cloudy sky and predict rain.

In contrast to the religious leaders who demanded a miraculous sign, when John the Baptist sent a messenger to Jesus to ask Him if He was the Messiah or if another person should be expected, Jesus replied, "The lame walk, the blind see, and the deaf hear" (*Luke 7:18-23*). This was enough to satisfy John who knew the Messianic prophecy of *Isaiah 35:5-6*. But it was not enough for the teachers of religious law who also knew Isaiah's prophecies and who still demanded a further sign.

As far as Jesus was concerned, the signs had already been given. And anyone who had knowledge of the scriptures should not only have identified Him as the Messiah, but should've been actively *expecting* Him just before His ministry began – much like the arrival of a rain cloud you can see on the horizon.

Why? Because the Book of Daniel foretold the *exact* time of the Messiah's arrival. The religious teachers knew this, and they were actively awaiting the Messiah. Yet, despite intimate knowledge of Daniel's prophecy and all the other Messianic prophecies, the religious leaders still rejected Jesus.

WAITING FOR THE MESSIAH

Before Jesus began His ministry, John the Baptist gained fame throughout Judea for His preaching, baptizing people in the Jordan River. Many people in Israel considered John to be a prophet, and the Jewish leaders came to Him and asked, "Are you the one we're expecting?" (*John 1:19*).

Who was it they were expecting? They were expecting the Messiah. The Jewish leaders were looking for the same prophet Moses predicted would rise up from among the people of Israel (*Deuteronomy 18:15-18*), and many speculated that John was that prophet. But John emphatically stated that he was *not* the Messiah.

The Jewish leaders then asked, "Well, if you're not the Messiah, are you Elijah?" (*John 1:21*). Why did they ask this? Because the prophet Malachi predicted that Elijah would precede the Messiah (*Malachi 4:5-6*).

So why were the Jewish leaders and priests interrogating John the Baptist and asking him all these questions about the Messiah? The answer is clear. They knew the scriptures, and they knew that the Messiah was predicted to appear at that *exact* moment in time.

DANIEL'S 483 YEARS

While still captive in Babylon, the prophet Daniel was visited by the angel Gabriel. During this visitation, Gabriel revealed that precisely 483 years would pass from the time the command is given to rebuild Jerusalem until "the Anointed One" comes (*Daniel 9:25*).

So what did this mean? It meant just what it says. It meant the Messiah (the Anointed One) would appear *exactly* 483 years after the command to rebuild Jerusalem. So, did this happen? To find out, we only need to count forward 483 years from the time of the command to rebuild Jerusalem.

457 B.C.

In the year 457 B.C., the King of Persia, Artaxerxes, issued a decree instructing officials in the province west of the Euphrates to give Ezra "whatever he requests of you" in his efforts to rebuild Jerusalem, reinstitute the Temple services, appoint judges and magistrates, and teach the Law (*Ezra 7:11-26*). This is the starting point for the 483 year countdown.

A.D. 27

If you count forward 483 years from 457 B.C., you get the year A.D. 27 (note that the year zero doesn't count). This is the time when Israel should have been looking for the arrival of the Messiah. And as we noted earlier, the chief priests and Jewish leaders of this era *were* looking for the Messiah, which is why they so avidly questioned John the Baptist.

The year A.D. 27 coincides with the beginning of the ministry of Jesus of Nazareth, since it's generally accepted that His ministry lasted 3 to 3.5 years, and He was crucified in spring of the year A.D. 31.

AFTER THE 483 YEARS

The Book of Daniel also predicts that after the 483 years pass and the Messiah comes, He will be killed "appearing to have accomplished nothing." Then a ruler will arise whose armies will destroy the Temple and the City (***Daniel 9:26***). So did this happen?

Yes. Jesus was killed, and His ministry appeared to have fallen short of its goals. Why? Because at the time of His arrival, the Israelites were looking for a Messiah who would conquer their Roman oppressors and rule the earth in righteousness forever. They were expecting fulfillment of the prophecies of the Messiah's **second coming**, not realizing at the time that the Messiah would come twice – once as a "suffering" Messiah and the second time as a "conquering" Messiah. So the death of Jesus on the cross seemed to indicate (at least in the world's eyes) that He was not the Messiah – that He had "accomplished nothing."

Less than four decades after the crucifixion (A.D. 70), the Roman legions under the command of Titus destroyed Jerusalem and the Temple. To this day, the Arch of Titus stands in Rome as a monument to this event. So was Titus "a ruler whose armies will destroy the Temple and the City"? Yes. While Titus was, at the time, commander of the military campaign to put down the Jewish rebellion, he was also the son of the Emperor Vespasian. And Titus himself served as Emperor following his father's death, making him "a ruler" in every sense of the word.

THE MESSIAH HAD TO LIVE BETWEEN A.D. 27 AND A.D. 70

The Book of Daniel clearly stated that the Messiah would come in the year A.D. 27 and the Temple would be destroyed shortly thereafter (which it was in A.D. 70). So in order to fulfill the Messianic prophecies of the Old Testament, any Messianic candidate would have to have lived between the years 27 and 70. Jesus of Nazareth is the only historical figure from this period (or any period) to fulfill the Messianic prophecies.

So either Jesus is the Messiah the Jewish leaders were expecting when they questioned John the Baptist, or the Messiah never appeared and never will appear. There can be no future Jewish Messiah, because the Messiah had to appear within this short historical timeframe in order fulfill the prophecy of Daniel 9:25.

So now we come full circle. If Jesus was a mere man attempting to arrange His life so it would appear He fulfilled the Messianic prophecies, how did He arrange the timing of His birth so He would be on earth between the years A.D. 27 and A.D. 70? Can you dictate the timing of your birth?

Coupled with His subsequent fulfillment of all the other Old Testament Messianic prophecies, the life of Jesus would have to be an astounding coincidence which defies all statistical probability. His generous odds of fulfilling *only* the Messianic prophecies from the last chapter were 1 in 137 billion, and modern historians estimate the total world population between A.D. 27 and A.D. 70 was somewhere between 200 and 300 million. So if you're betting against Jesus as the Messiah, you're really making a totally irrational bet against all odds. Good luck with that.

But again, don't take my word for it. Read the Bible for yourself. It reveals who Jesus is. In fact, if you're still not sure, examine His own words. Jesus will gladly tell you exactly who He is.

CHAPTER 6
WHO JESUS SAID HE WAS

"You will see one like the Son of Man coming on the clouds of Heaven."

— Mark 14:62 (NLT)

YOU ALREADY KNOW what I think. But who did Jesus say He was? That's the question you need to ask.

Many people are quick to say that Jesus never claimed to be the Messiah. But if you read the scriptures in context, you'll see this just isn't the case. So why does this view continue to spread? Unfortunately, it's because many people just haven't read the Bible.

Despite the fact you can find the Bible almost everywhere in modern society, few people actually read it anymore. As a result, most people form their opinions about the Bible based on what other people have told them. And oftentimes, those people haven't read the Bible either! See why I've been encouraging you to read the Bible for yourself? Don't let others draw conclusions for you – not when it comes to such an important issue.

Many years ago when I was in college, a good friend of mine did exactly this. She made an offhand remark, and I'm sure she was just repeating something she heard somewhere else. Here's what she said "Well, Jesus never claimed to be the Messiah. Other people only said He did." I couldn't believe this was true, but off the top of my head, I couldn't dispute what she said. I didn't have a Bible with me, and I probably wouldn't have known where to look if I did. Is that because such a passage wasn't there? No. The passages were there. I just didn't know them well enough at the time to point out the inaccuracy and explain those passages.

So while I firmly believed Jesus was the Messiah, I considered the idea that maybe she was right. Maybe I had put words in the mouth of Jesus that just weren't there. But rather than take her word for it, I decided to check for myself. I turned to the authoritative sources on statements made by Jesus – Matthew, Mark, Luke, and John. And, after I re-read these books, I could understand why this myth was able to spread. If you read the Gospels, you'll struggle to find a passage where Jesus specifically states the exact words, "I am the Messiah." Still, to say that He didn't believe this or relay this message to others is completely dishonest.

Why do I say this? Because if you read the Gospels in context – with full understanding of the Messianic prophecies and what the language used by Jesus meant to 1st Century Israelites – then you'll know without a doubt that Jesus proclaimed Himself to be the Messiah over and over and over again on multiple occasions.

But again, don't take my word for it. Read the Bible firsthand. If you don't, you can be easily misled in regard to what's in it. Thinking Jesus never claimed to be the Messiah is a prime example. Because below are a few instances where Jesus did exactly that.

THE WOMAN AT THE WELL

While traveling through Samaria on His way to Galilee, Jesus and His disciples stopped at the village of Sychar. Tired, Jesus sat down next to Jacob's well and struck up a conversation with a woman who had come to draw water. After asking Him a number of questions, she said, "When the Messiah comes, I know He will explain everything to us." What was Jesus' response? He told her, "I am He" (*John 4:25-26*).

Did you catch that? Jesus said, "I am He" in response to her remark, "when the Messiah comes." So, yes, *technically* the exact words, "I am the Messiah" didn't come out of His mouth. But would you really interpret His response as anything less than that?

By itself, this is enough to put an end to the idea that Jesus never claimed to be the Messiah, but it's not the only instance. There are plenty more.

JESUS CLAIMS TO BE THE SON OF GOD

While in the Temple, the people surrounded Jesus and demanded that He tell them whether or not He was the Messiah. As part of His reply, Jesus said, "The Father and I are one." This prompted the people to pick up stones to kill Him. Jesus then asked them, "In my Father's name, I have done many good works. For which of these are you going to stone me?" And the crowd replied, "Not for any good work, but for blasphemy, because you – a mere man – claim to be God" (*John 10:24-33*).

Jesus claimed to be much more than a prophet. He claimed to be God in the flesh. What else do you think He meant when He said, "The Father and I are one"? Clearly, He was saying, "God and Myself are one and the same." And that's what the crowds heard. Otherwise, why would they accuse Him of claiming to be God? And why would they try to stone Him for it?

JESUS SAID HE LIVED BEFORE ABRAHAM

When the crowds asked Jesus who He was and how He could say that Abraham (who died more than 2,000 years earlier) had looked forward to Jesus' coming, Jesus replied, "Before Abraham was, I AM." When He said this, the crowds picked up stones to stone Him (*John 8:58*).

Why did they pick up stones to stone Him? Again, it's because Jesus proclaimed Himself God. Jesus didn't say, "I AM" because He was getting all philosophical and asserting His existence. Jesus was making a bold statement. Claiming to be "I AM" was quite significant in 1st Century Israel (or anytime for that matter). Why? Because when God appeared to Moses in a burning bush, He identified Himself as "I AM" (*Exodus 3:14*). And Jesus identified

Himself as the same "I AM" from the burning bush. He was saying that He was the God of Israel who led the Hebrews out of Egyptian bondage – that He existed before Abraham did. To many people, this was outrageous, and that's why they tried to stone Him.

JESUS SAID "IN ME, YOU HAVE SEEN THE FATHER"

When Jesus said, "from now on you know the Father and have seen Him," Philip replied, "Lord, show us the Father, and we will believe." Then Jesus asked him, "Philip, have I been with you all this time and you still don't you know me? If you have seen me, then you have seen the Father, for I am in the Father and the Father is in me" (*John 14:8-11*).

Did you catch that? Jesus said, "If you have seen me, then you have seen the Father." He didn't say, "Trust me, I've seen the Father. He exists." He said, "*You* have seen Him." Jesus was claiming to be the physical manifestation of God – God the Father in the flesh.

Jesus reiterated this when He told the crowds, "If you trust me, you trust the God who sent me. For when you look at me, you are looking at the One who sent me" (*John 12:45*).

When I first started reading the Bible, this is a concept I just didn't grasp. Initially, I thought of Jesus as distinct from God the Father, much like a human father and son are related, but separate people. But one day, when I was reading this passage, a light bulb went off. I finally realized who Jesus really was – God in the flesh! (Yes, I know. You already knew that. But remember, I'm a little slow here). But the important thing is that I eventually caught on, so I guess I shouldn't feel too bad. After all, Philip spent every day with Jesus for three years before he figured it out!

THE SCRIPTURES POINT TO ME

Jesus said, "You search the scriptures because you think they give you eternal life, but the scriptures point to me!" (*John 5:39*). The entire Bible centers around God's relationship with man, so when Jesus says, "the scriptures point to me," He's clearly stating He's more than "just a man."

Later, Jesus reaffirms this statement. After the resurrection, two followers of Jesus were walking to the village of Emmaus when Jesus suddenly appeared and began walking with them. While walking with them, He said, "Wasn't it clearly predicted that the Messiah would have to suffer all these things before entering His glory?" Then Jesus explained the writings of Moses and all the prophets, revealing in the Scriptures the things concerning Himself (*Luke 24:13-27*). Notice that Jesus didn't say the "things concerning God," but the "things concerning Himself."

EQUAL WITH GOD

When Jesus healed a man on the Sabbath, the Jewish leaders criticized Him for it. He replied to them by saying, "My Father is always working, and so am I." In response, the Jewish leaders tried all the harder to kill Him, because He called God His Father, making Himself equal to God (*John 5:16-18*). The Jewish leaders understood Jesus clearly. He was equating Himself to God in what they viewed as a violation of the 1st Commandment – "You must not have any god but me" (*Exodus 20:3*). If Jesus believed Himself anything less than the Messiah – God in the flesh – He would have known He was in violation of this commandment.

MANY WILL COME IN MY NAME

When the disciples asked Jesus to explain what signs would signal His return and the end of the age, one of things Jesus said is that "many will come in my name, claiming, '*I am the Messiah*,' and they will deceive many" (*Matthew 24:4-5*). Here, Jesus is essentially telling the disciples, "Since I'm the Messiah, one sign of the end will be the appearance of false messiahs who will claim, '*I am the Messiah*'." If Jesus didn't believe Himself to be the Messiah, then wouldn't He have told His disciples to look for signs related to the true Messiah? He would have. But instead, He told them to ignore **anyone** who claimed to be the Messiah. Why? Because He alone was the Messiah.

JESUS AGREED WITH PETER

When Jesus asked the disciples who they thought He was, Peter said He was the Messiah – the Son of the Living God. Jesus responded by applauding Peter, saying "You are blessed, Simon Peter, Son of John, because My Father in heaven has revealed this to you. You did not learn this from any human being" (*Matthew 16:15-17*). Jesus didn't say, "Wrong, Peter. I'm not the Messiah. I'm just a prophet." Just the opposite. Jesus agreed with Peter's assertion that He was the Messiah and blessed him for it.

JESUS ACCEPTED WORSHIP

Jesus repeatedly accepted worship from others without rebuke, an act which would be blasphemy for a mere man since worship is reserved for God alone.

Need some examples? After Jesus walked on water, the disciples worshipped Him and called Him, "the Son of God" (*Matthew 14:33*). When Mary and Mary Magdalene left the empty tomb, they encountered Jesus, grabbed His feet, and worshipped Him (*Matthew 28:9-10*). A man with leprosy knelt before Jesus and called Him, "Lord" (*Matthew 8:2*), and a blind man healed by Jesus worshipped Him (*John 9:38*).

The Gospel accounts mention numerous instances where Jesus was worshipped, but not once did Jesus ever tell anyone to stop. In fact, several times throughout the Bible, men fall down in worship of angels who say, "Stop! Worship is reserved for God alone." By saying nothing and accepting worship, Jesus is revealing His true identity.

COMING ON THE CLOUDS OF HEAVEN

When charged with blasphemy before the High Council, the high priest demanded that Jesus reveal whether or not He was the Messiah. Jesus replied, "You will see one like the Son of Man coming on the clouds of heaven" (*Matthew 26:64*). So what does this mean? This is a direct reference to a Messianic prophecy in the Book of Daniel (*Daniel 7:13*). So who is this "Son of Man" prophesied in Daniel? If you keep reading, you'll find out that He is given authority, honor, and power over all the nations of the world, so that everyone in the world will obey Him. His rule is eternal and His kingdom never ending (***Daniel 7:14***). Jesus claimed to be this prophesied ruler.

SHARING GOD'S GLORY?

Jesus also told His disciples, "Now, the time has come for the Son of Man to enter His glory" (***John 12:23-29***). Jesus said this knowing that God does not share His glory with anyone. For God said, "I will give my glory to no one, nor share my praise with carved idols" (***Isaiah 42:8***). Was God lying? No. Did Jesus lie or engage in blasphemy when He talked about entering into His glory? No. Why? Because He and the Father are one and the same.

THE RIGHT HAND OF GOD

Also while He was before the High Council, Jesus was asked, "Are you the Messiah?" He replied, "From now on, the Son of Man will be seated in the place of power at God's right hand" (***Luke 22:69***). What did He mean by this? Jesus was quoting King David who said, "The Lord said to my Lord, sit in the place of honor at my right hand" (***Psalm 110:1***).

How can the Lord sit in the place of honor at His own right hand? How is it possible that Jesus is both Son of Man and Son of God? If He's God in the flesh, who is the Father? These are all good questions. The way I would explain it is this – if I put my hand in an aquarium, my hand is me, but my hand is not *all* of me. Yet my hand moves only at my direction, and anything my hand does is something I do.

So Jesus is essentially the hand of God in the form of a human. By Himself, He's not *all* of God, but He's still God. Just as your right hand represents you, but isn't *all* of you. And this is how Jesus described Himself – as the right hand of God.

And Jesus made many other statements not listed here in which He claimed to be the Messiah or God in the flesh. For instance, Jesus claimed to be "the way and the truth and the life" (***John 14:6***) and "the bread of life" (***John 6:35***).

THE CHARACTERISTICS OF GOD

As I came to the realization of who Jesus really was and is, it occurred to me that the Gospels should corroborate Jesus' claims about His true identity. In other words, if Jesus is God in the flesh, then the narratives of His life should provide evidence that He exhibited the characteristics you would expect of God. So did He?

Some of the college religion and philosophy classes I took noted that God has certain universal characteristics. So I decided to take a look at those and see if Jesus still measured up. Here's what I found.

Omnipotence – By definition, God is all-powerful – meaning He has power over all things in the universe. Is there any evidence Jesus was all-powerful? History says, "yes."

According to the Old Testament, only God has the power to forgive sins (*Jeremiah 31:24*). Yet, Jesus boldly declared His own power to forgive sins, revealing Himself as God (*Mark 2:5-11*). While speaking to a crowd, Jesus claimed the power to lay down His life and pick it up again (*John 10:17-18*). The resurrection confirmed He has this power (*John 20:11-18*).

Jesus also displayed His power over the wind and waves when He made the storm stop on the lake (*Luke 8:24-25*). Jesus commanded fish and they obeyed (*John 21:6*). He cast Roman soldiers to the ground with nothing more than the breath of His mouth (*John 18:6*), and He also walked on water (*Mark 6:48-49*).

At His command, diseases were cured (*Mark 1:40-42*), the blind could see (*Matthew 9:27-30*), and the paralyzed could walk (*John 5:5-17*).

Presented with these examples, you have to conclude that such a person is omnipotent. After all, if you can heal the blind, walk on water, and raise the dead – what *can't* you do?

Omnipresence – God is also omnipresent. He's everywhere at all times. He exists in all places in the past, present, and future. Can this be said of Jesus? Is there any evidence of His omnipresence? Yes. There is.

When they first met, Jesus stated that He saw Nathanael under the fig tree earlier that day. His statement mesmerized Nathanael, who recognized this as knowledge that no other man could have (*John 1:47-51*). Yet Jesus was there.

The Gospel of John tells us that the Spirit of God became flesh and took the name of Jesus. He existed in the beginning with God, and He was God (*John 1:1-2*).

Jesus assured His disciples He would always be with them, even to the end of the age (*Matthew 28:20*), and Paul testified that Jesus "fills all things everywhere with himself" (*Ephesians 1:23*).

Omniscience – God is all-knowing. There isn't a thing under the sun that He doesn't know. He not only knows everything that we've done, but our thoughts and motives as well. So did Jesus show any indication of this ability? Absolutely.

Upon meeting a Samaritan woman, Jesus told her everything she had ever done (*John 4:39*). His knowledge was so detailed, it alone convinced her He was the Messiah.

The disciples, who spent more time with Jesus during His earthly ministry than anyone else, testified that He knows *everything* (*John 16:30*) – the very definition of omniscience.

As a young boy, Jesus and His family made a pilgrimage to the Temple in Jerusalem. While there, Jesus amazed the Jewish religious teachers with His understanding and His answers (*Luke 2:46-47*). As an adult, Jesus taught in the Temple, and the people were amazed at the depth of His knowledge, saying "How does He know all this?" since He was not a man educated and trained by men (*John 7:14-15*).

Jesus even illustrated His knowledge of the most minute details of creation when He told Peter to catch a fish, open its mouth, and find a large silver coin inside (*Matthew 17:27*).

Jesus knew Lazarus was dead, even when His disciples still thought Lazarus was just sick (*John 11:14*). Jesus also had prior knowledge of His betrayal by one of the disciples (*John 6:70-71*), and complete knowledge that

He would suffer at the hands of the Jewish authorities, die, and rise from the dead (*Matthew 16:21*).

Eternal – Yet another characteristic of God is His eternal nature. God is not bound by time or death. According to the Old Testament, God is "the First and the Last. There is no other God" (*Isaiah 44:6*).

Is there any evidence Jesus was eternal in nature? The Apostle John testified yes when he fell at the feet of a resurrected Jesus who assured Him, "Don't be afraid! I am the First and the Last. I am alive forever" (*Revelation 1:17*).

In addition, Paul says that Jesus "existed before anything else" (*Colossians 1:17*), and he described Jesus as being "the same yesterday, today, and tomorrow" *forever* (*Hebrews 13:8*).

In a Messianic prophecy, the prophet Micah claimed this future ruler of Israel will come out of Bethlehem, and His "origins are from the distant past" (*Micah 5:2*). And the prophet Isaiah described the Messiah (the great light who would appear in Galilee) as "Everlasting Father" (*Isaiah 9:6*). Both of these Messianic prophecies were fulfilled by Jesus, so it stands to reason that He is the "Everlasting Father whose origins are from the distant past."

Jesus Displays The Characteristics of God

Are these the only characteristics of God? No. After all, we're talking about God's traits here – who really knows what they all are? We could spend an entire lifetime debating the subject and splitting hairs. But ask yourself just one question: What would you expect God to be like?

Think about that. What picture forms in your mind. Wouldn't you expect God to say, "Come to me all who are heavy burdened, and I'll give you rest" (*Matthew 11:28*)? Wouldn't you expect God to say, "Let he who is without sin cast the first stone" (*John 8:7*)? Wouldn't you expect God to say, "Love your enemies" (*Matthew 5:44*), "blessed are the peacemakers" (*Matthew 5:9*), and "I am the way, the truth, and the life" (*John 14:6*). Wouldn't you expect God to walk on water, heal the blind, and raise the dead? You would. And guess what? Your imagination paints a picture of the living, breathing Jesus.

Think of any characteristic you would expect God to display, and I bet you'll find an example where Jesus displays that same characteristic. The crowds surrounding Jesus in the Temple put it best. They asked, "When the Messiah comes, will He do greater things than this man?" (*John 7:31*).

THE TRUTH ABOUT JESUS

Jesus knew the scriptures like no one else. Remember, when He was 12 years old, Jesus met with the religious teachers in the Temple, and they were amazed with His knowledge and understanding (*Luke 2:46-47*). Jesus knew *exactly* what He was saying when He proclaimed, "I AM" and "You will see One who looks like the Son of Man coming on the clouds of heaven." He clearly understood these words and phrases as references to the Messiah – God in the flesh.

Furthermore, He allowed others to worship Him, and He constantly equated Himself to the God of Israel. Are these the words and actions of someone who views Himself as an ordinary man? Are these the words of just one in a long line of prophets? Why do you think the Pharisees and Sadducees were constantly accusing Him of blasphemy? It's because He, a mere man in their eyes, claimed to be equal to God.

Plenty of people say Jesus never claimed to be the Messiah, but the position of Jesus Himself is clear and unequivocal. Those who say He was a great moral teacher, but not God in the flesh, ignore His actual teachings. If you believe Jesus is not the Son of God, then you can't also believe He's a great moral teacher. How could you if He's proclaiming to be someone He's not? If you don't think He's the Son of God, then you have to believe He's either crazy or a liar – but you can't straddle the fence and believe that He's "good."

Only three options really exist. Jesus either lied about who He was, was deluded about who He was, or He was who He said He was. But again, don't take my word for it. For one thing, you don't have to. Many witnesses who spent time with Jesus were beaten, ridiculed, and martyred for their insistence that Jesus was who He said He was, and their testimony is a lot more compelling than mine. So why not take the time to investigate what they said?

CHAPTER 7
EYE WITNESSES

"God raised Jesus from the dead, and we are all witnesses of this... So let everyone in Israel know for certain that God has made this Jesus, whom you crucified, to be both Lord and Messiah."

— Acts 2:32,36 (NLT)

THROUGHOUT HISTORY AND right up to the present day, we often convict people – sometimes sentence them to death – based solely on eyewitness testimony. Of course, the more credible the witness, the more weight his testimony carries.

You just read what Jesus said about Himself. But who did others say Jesus was? In my pursuit of truth, this is a question I examined with great interest. After all, firsthand testimony will either verify or contradict the claims of Jesus and form a picture of His true identity. In fact, Jesus Himself said, "If I testify on behalf of myself, my words mean nothing" (*John 5:31*). Jesus then identified two witnesses – God the Father and John the Baptist – as qualified to speak on His behalf. So who did they say He was?

God the Father testified that Jesus was the Messiah through His teachings, His miracles, His fulfillment of all the Old Testament Messianic prophecies, and His resurrection. Also, after John baptized Jesus in the Jordan

River, a voice from heaven said, "You are my dearly beloved Son, bringing me great joy" (*Mark 1:11*).

John the Baptist also testified that Jesus was the Messiah, the Son of God. Why is this important? Because the people of Israel, including many of the religious leaders, regarded John as a prophet (*Matthew 11:9*). Remember, the leading priests and religious officials even approached John and asked him if *he* was the Messiah – that's how highly regarded John was (*John 1:19-28*).

So who did John say Jesus was? John called Jesus "the Lamb of God who takes away the sin of the world" (*John 1:29*). He also said, when God sent him to baptize with water, He told him the Holy Spirit would descend like a dove from heaven and rest upon the One who would baptize with the Holy Spirit. John then said, "I saw this happen to Jesus, and I testify that He is the Chosen One of God" (*John 1:32-34*).

Both John the Baptist and God the Father corroborate Jesus' story. But what did His contemporaries say? Was Jesus regarded as the Messiah by those who knew Him best? Let's investigate.

THE APOSTLES

My freshman year in college, I read a book titled *More Than A Carpenter* by Josh McDowell. This book further strengthened my already iron clad faith in Jesus Christ. It presented the post-resurrection reaction of the apostles as proof that Jesus was the Messiah – an argument I had never really considered before.

Remember, when I first read the Bible I wasn't quite sure if it was truly the Word of God. Maybe it was, maybe it wasn't. Christians certainly said it was. But where was the evidence? Then I encountered the hundreds of fulfilled prophecies in the Bible, and those prophecies convinced me that the Bible really was the Word of God. Reading *More Than A Carpenter* (which I recommend you do) opened my eyes to additional evidence – the eyewitness testimony of Jesus' closest disciples.

Now, I know what you're probably thinking – of course, the apostles claim Jesus was the Messiah. They were His devoted followers for years, and they fanatically embraced all His teachings. What else would they say? That He was a fraud? That they wasted a good part of their lives following a false prophet?

Like you, I initially embraced this same line of thinking. After all, history books are filled with stories of false prophets and messiahs with devoted followers convinced beyond all doubt that their guy was God's messenger. And many of these people were so convinced – so certain – that they died for those beliefs. You can probably think of quite a few modern day examples of cult leaders who actually convinced their followers to commit suicide.

But there's something that separates Jesus from all of history's cult leaders – something even beyond the fulfilled Old Testament prophecies. What is this great differentiator?

The resurrection.

The apostles personally witnessed the crucifixion of Jesus. They watched Him die, and they mourned His death. Then, in a matter of days, they started zealously and publicly preaching that Jesus rose from the dead. But why?

Before you answer, ask yourself another question – who did the apostles think Jesus was? We tend to make the mistake of projecting our own views on these men. But the perception of Jesus among modern Christians is far different from that of the closest followers of Jesus prior to His crucifixion and resurrection.

In first century Israel, Messianic fever was rampant. Remember, the scriptures predicted the Messiah would appear sometime shortly after A.D. 27. So the Jewish people were actively anticipating and awaiting the arrival of the Messiah. And they did not expect the Messiah they were waiting for to be crucified. No. Not at all. They had a much different idea. The Messiah would come as a great conqueror and king, throwing off the oppressive yoke of Rome and liberating the nation.

The idea of a suffering Messiah sacrificed to cleanse the world of sin was a totally foreign concept. This is why the apostles repeatedly refused to listen to Jesus when He told them what would happen to Him (***Matthew 16:21-23***). The apostles had devoted their lives to the idea that Jesus was not only the Messiah, but also this – that the Messiah would be a great political leader who would rule the nation of Israel and the entire world (and one day He will. It just wasn't at that moment). So you can imagine how crushed they were when they saw Jesus crucified.

Their Messiah was dead. How could this be? After all, the scriptures said the Messiah would live forever. At the time, the only reasonable conclusion they could draw was they must have been mistaken in thinking Jesus was the Messiah. With the death of Jesus came the depressing realization that everything they had devoted their lives to for three entire years had been a lie. They even refused to believe Mary Magdalene when she told them about the empty tomb. They did not expect Jesus to rise from the dead. In fact, they were so sure of His death, they "grieved and wept" (*Mark 16:10*).

So what led to such a dramatic change in such a short period of time? What transformed the apostles from weeping followers of a dead prophet to confident preachers in the rise of a resurrected Messiah? Only two possibilities exist – either they saw the resurrected Jesus or they hatched a coordinated conspiracy to lie and say they did. And if you really think about it, you'll realize that the latter possibility isn't realistic at all.

WHY WOULD THEY LIE?

Now, it may be perfectly reasonable to expect that the apostles might lie about the resurrection. After all, as we've already noted, history shows us that a number of cult leaders and their followers have lied for various reasons – fame, money, power, an inflated sense of self-importance, a deluded belief that a lie is reality, etc.

But when I examined them, I found that not one of these reasons applied to disciples. Don't want to take my word for it? I don't blame you, so let's take a look at the possibilities.

Fame, Money, and Power – Today, I wouldn't consider it a stretch at all for a follower of a dead person to claim their spiritual leader rose from the dead. Because in today's world of religious tolerance, such a person could easily build the support of a small, devoted group of followers more than willing to shower that person with adulation, money, and power. So the incentive structure exists for such a thing to take place. In fact, our modern society encourages it, and we can all cite examples of charlatans, both past and present, who have taken advantage of the easily misled.

But again, we shouldn't make the mistake of assuming the apostles faced a world remotely similar to our present day reality and environment. Their world was quite different. Preaching the resurrection of Jesus did not translate into fame, money, and power. Instead, it led to nothing but condemnation, persecution, and martyrdom.

The apostles didn't achieve fame and recognition in their day, only infamy and disdain. They were banished from the synagogue and Jewish society in general. They were hunted and persecuted for their beliefs. They endured hunger, beatings, stoning, imprisonment, and exposure to the elements. Fame certainly didn't offer any incentive to endure such misery. Would you tell a lie over and over again if it resulted in such treatment? Of course you wouldn't.

So what about wealth? Did the apostles reap great wealth by spreading the Gospel of Jesus? No. Most of them lived lives of utter poverty, totally reliant on odd jobs or the charity of strangers for their day-to-day livelihood. Would you tell a lie over and over again if it resulted in nothing but a life of poverty? Of course you wouldn't.

How about power? Did the apostles rise to great positions of power as a result of preaching the Good News? No. Far from it. Instead, society ostracized them. While Christians (a small minority of people at the time) held them in high regard, this high regard didn't translate into wealth or fame or power. And even if it had, they probably wouldn't have accepted it anyway. Why? Because each one of the apostles lived a life of humility, constantly denigrating himself while elevating Jesus. So the pursuit of power certainly wasn't an incentive to tell a lie over and over again.

So if the apostles didn't receive fame, money, or power, what *did* they receive as a result of preaching the Gospel of Jesus Christ throughout what was then the known world? Here's what they received – relentless persecution and death. In fact, every apostle except John died a horrible, tortuous death. Here's what happened to each of them:

Simon (Peter) – crucified upside down

Andrew – crucified

James – beheaded

John – died a natural death while in exile

Philip – crucified

Bartholomew (Nathanael) – crucified

Thomas – speared

Matthew – speared

James, Son of Alphaeus – stoned

Thaddaeus – stoned

Simon the Zealot – crucified

Ten of the eleven remaining disciples of Jesus were executed for their testimony that He was the Messiah – that He was crucified, died, and rose on the third day. Would you walk from town to town telling other people what you know is an outright lie if all it got you was a lifetime of condemnation and persecution, topped off with a tortuous death? Me neither. But some people would like us to believe that's exactly what the apostles did. But I'm not one of them. I find another scenario much more likely. In fact, it's a rather simple explanation. Are you ready for it?

Okay, here it is… *Maybe they were telling the truth*. Maybe the reason they preached the Gospel despite the terrible consequences is because they actually saw, touched, and talked to the resurrected Jesus.

An Inflated Sense of Self-Importance – If the apostles didn't receive fame, money, or power, maybe they had another motive. After all, I did mention that Christians, even though they were a small minority at the time, held the apostles in high regard. So maybe the apostles were motivated by the inflated sense of self-importance they received from preaching the Gospel and having been personal companions of Jesus?

This certainly sounds reasonable at first, but when you start to examine the evidence, it just doesn't add up. Because if the apostles wanted to focus on themselves and their own greatness as firsthand witnesses of the risen Christ, then they certainly did a poor job. They constantly talked about their own shortcomings, and they retold and perpetuated stories about themselves that were, at the very least, unflattering.

For instance, all the apostles scattered like cowards when Jesus was arrested (*Mark 14:50*). Peter, who said he would die for Jesus, then denied Him three times in His hour of need less than a day later (*Luke 22:54-62*). If the Gospel of Jesus is a lie hatched by the apostles, wouldn't they push a story and write letters that portrayed themselves as loyal, devoted, and courageous servants? I would think so. But they didn't. Instead, they openly admitted to their faults and failures, almost to the point of boasting about them. Who would do such a thing unless it was the truth?

When all the other apostles told Thomas they had seen the resurrected Christ, what was his response? Did he say, "That's great. I believe you." Far from it. Thomas didn't believe them at all. Instead, he said, "Unless I put my fingers in the holes in His hands and feet and put my hand in the hole in His side, I won't believe it" (*John 20:25*). A short time later, Jesus appeared to Thomas and invited him to see the scars and touch the hole in His side.

Now, think about it. If the story of the resurrection is nothing more than a conspiracy hatched by the apostles, would Thomas agree to this account which paints him in such an unfavorable light? Would he agree to single himself out as the only one who didn't believe? Human nature tells us he would not. The only logical explanation is that his story is the truth.

And who was the first person to see the resurrected Jesus? Was it Peter? Was it John? No. It was Mary Magdalene, and she immediately went and told the apostles that she had seen Jesus (*Mark 16:9-11*). Did they believe her? No. They didn't. This is a story that once again presents the apostles as men of little belief, doubting Mary's account of the resurrection, even though Jesus Himself told them He would rise again after three days. Why invent a story that puts you in such a negative light?

And what about the first witnesses at the empty tomb? Who were they?

They were three women – Mary Magdalene, Mary mother of James, and Salome (*Mark 16:1-4*). If the apostles had conspired to lie, would they concoct a story that placed three women at the empty tomb before themselves?

Remember, at this point in time, society considered women second-class citizens. To perpetuate a story where three women saw the glory of the empty tomb first and relayed their story to a bunch of men who didn't believe them, once again portrays the apostles in a negative light among the audience of their time. Such a story wouldn't generate the respect of peers, public adoration, or an inflated sense of self-importance. So why tell it? Again, the only reasonable explanation is they told the truth.

True Belief In A Lie – Another line of thinking that seems to make sense at first goes something like this, "Okay, so maybe the apostles didn't have a self-serving motive for preaching the Gospel. Maybe they were completely sincere, but deluded. Maybe they truly believed Jesus was the Messiah and they were just wrong. Happens all the time, right?"

I'll agree that some people can spend an entire lifetime believing a lie is the truth. But what if you *know* something is untrue? Would you go to your death insisting it's the truth? Probably not. So why is it believable to think that eleven different people would agree to do just that? It's not, and for me, that forms the foundation for one of the most powerful arguments in favor of Jesus and His resurrection. What is this powerful argument? It's this:

> *"The apostles witnessed the crucifixion of Jesus*
> *firsthand, and **they saw Him die.**"*

Unlike many religious zealots who simply believed in something or hoped in something without cause, the apostles *knew* what happened to Jesus. They saw Him hanging on the cross. They saw his side pierced. They saw him dead.

Certainly history is littered with the bodies of those who willingly chose death rather than compromise their beliefs. But those people acted on blind faith. They were never presented with decisive evidence proving their beliefs were wrong.

For the apostles, this wasn't the case. They dedicated their lives to the belief Jesus was the Messiah, and then they watched as He died on the cross. Afterward, they fell into an immediate state of depression, grieving and mourning the death of the man they had followed for three years. Clearly, they viewed His death as permanent.

Then something strange happened. In a matter of days, the apostles transformed from devastated and broken to joyful and confident. They started preaching to everyone who would listen that Jesus was and is the Messiah, that He had risen from the dead. Is that because in those few days, they put their heads together and hatched an elaborate conspiracy to lie? Is it because they needed a few days to concoct their stories and get them straight?

Believe that if you wish, but it doesn't make much sense. After all, if they were lying, then every single one of them *knew* it was all a lie. And what did they get in return for those "lies"? Condemnation, torture, persecution, and eventual violent death. So where's the incentive to lie? What's the motive? If it was all a lie, wouldn't it seem likely that *at least one* of the apostles would've recanted?

I think that's highly likely. After all, what are the odds of getting a group of eleven people to agree to tell the same lie in exchange for persecution and death? Not very good. And that's why the apostles' reaction to the crucifixion of Jesus is one the strongest pieces of evidence for believing He was and is who He said He was. But the apostles weren't the only ones. Many others made the bold claim that Jesus rose from the dead, and not one of them had any motive or incentive for doing so outside of simply telling the truth.

OTHER POST-RESURRECTION WITNESSES

Jesus also appeared to two followers who were en route to Emmaus, a small village seven miles outside of Jerusalem (*Luke 24:13-34*). And Jesus also appeared to a gathering of more than 500 followers at one time (*1 Corinthians 15:6*).

These witnesses faced the same level of persecution and condemnation as the apostles, yet they were just as fanatical in their insistence that Jesus was the Messiah – even though they also saw Him die on the cross. Why? Only the resurrection can explain it.

One believer, a man named Stephen, certainly knew that Jesus had died on the cross. When he was brought before the Jewish Council on false charges of blasphemy, he accused them of betraying and murdering the Messiah (*Acts 7:52*). He then testified he saw the resurrected Jesus standing in heaven at the right hand of God (*Acts 7:55-56*). Why would he do this unless it was the truth? It certainly didn't get him fame, fortune, power, or worldly gain of any sort. Instead, a crowd dragged Stephen out of the City and stoned him. Yet, as he died, Stephen asked Jesus to receive his spirit and forgive those who were stoning him (*Acts 7:58-60*). Do those sound like the dying words of a man devoted to anything less than the truth?

Yet, believe it or not, there's another witness I found far more convincing than Stephen and all of the apostles put together. In fact, as Stephen was stoned, the same people who threw the stones took off their coats and laid them at the feet of this man. A devout Jew and Pharisee, he set out to extinguish the Gospel of Jesus Christ from the face of the earth. And you know what? In doing so, he became the one witness who solidified my belief more than any other.

GOD'S SUPER WITNESS

Who was this super-witness for Jesus Christ? His name was Saul, and he was a man like no other in first century Israel. A Jew from the tribe of Benjamin. A Pharisee. Highly educated. He was a Roman citizen, meaning he had beneficial legal status in regard to laws, property, and governance within the Empire (*Acts 22:24-29*). He spoke Greek and Hebrew, and he was well-versed in classical literature and Stoic philosophy. He studied under Gamaliel, one of the most noted rabbis in the history of Judaism. He had status, knowledge, access, wealth, connections, and worldly approval.

But in spite of all of this, what was Saul most noted for? He was most famous for his violent persecution of the early church. Saul hated Christians with a passion unmatched by his peers. In fact, he built quite a reputation among the followers of Jesus as one of the foremost enemies of the faith.

If there was any man in ancient Israel who lacked motive and incentive for proclaiming the Gospel, it was Saul. After all, why would a man who hated Christians with such zealous fervor choose to become one of them? What would he have to gain? If the early Christians had incentive to lie about the resurrection (and they didn't), what would be Saul's reason? He already had respect, position, high standing, and worldly acceptance. Why would he turn on every principle he held so dear, embrace the faith he so vehemently sought to extinguish, and in the process, give up an accumulated lifetime of status, wealth, and worldly position?

Yet, in the blink of an eye, that's exactly what he did. Saul transformed from the most murderous Christian assassin of his time into the greatest evangelist for Jesus Christ the world has ever known. The question I asked myself, and you should ask yourself, is this... *Why?*

THE ROAD TO DAMASCUS

After the stoning of Stephen, the Book of Acts tells us that Saul went from house to house in Jerusalem, throwing Christian believers into prison. Then he went to the high priest and requested to have letters addressed to the synagogues in Damascus so he could arrest the Christians he found there and bring them back to Jerusalem in chains (*Acts 9:1-2*). With every breath, Saul threatened to kill the Christians. He hated them, and his goal was nothing less than to exterminate them. But in an instant, all that changed. Something radically changed Saul's life and the entire Christian movement – *literally overnight*.

Saul not only stopped persecuting Christians, he became one. And he didn't just become a run-of-the-mill, ho-hum believer. He transformed into one of the most passionate advocates for Jesus Christ who ever walked on earth. And all this happened in a matter of hours! What could possibly have occurred to account for such a radical transformation?

I believe there's one answer and one answer only: *Saul saw the resurrected Jesus.*

Fortunately, we don't have to speculate because the Bible tells us exactly what happened. According to the Book of Acts, while en route to Damascus to round up the Christians, a bright light enveloped Saul and a voice from heaven said, "Saul, Saul. Why are you persecuting me?" When Saul inquired as to who he was persecuting, the voice replied, "I am Jesus, the one you are persecuting" (*Acts 9:3-9*).

While this story is quickly discounted by many people who don't believe in God or supernatural events, it seems to me to be the most logical explanation for Saul's conversion. After all, what else could explain his dramatic transformation, other than the truth of what the Bible claims? How many people do you know who have made such wholesale changes to their deeply held religious beliefs in a mere matter of hours? Not many I would wager. In fact, you probably don't know anyone who fits this description. I know I don't. But again, that's exactly what happened to Saul. Don't you find that strange? I do.

From then on, Saul (now known as Paul) spent his life passionately preaching in favor of the very thing he had marshaled all his strength and energy to destroy, saying such things as, "Jesus Christ rose from the dead" (*1 Corinthians 15:3-4*) and "In Jesus is all the complete fullness of God in a human form" (*Colossians 2:9*). Paul didn't just make a few off-hand remarks. He truly performed a complete and total one hundred eighty degree turn. He gave up everything from his previous life in order to tell others about Jesus, spending the remainder of his life eating, sleeping, and breathing the Gospel of Christ. He preached in an untold number of cities, covering the entire Mediterranean from Jerusalem to Rome. He wrote 13 of the 27 books of the New Testament, and he consistently put his life on the line to spread the Good News. Why would he do *any of this* unless the Bible's account of his conversion experience is the absolute truth?

What Paul Sacrificed

Don't think this is such a big deal? Think this was easy for Paul? Think again. What Paul sacrificed to preach the Gospel of Christ speaks volumes. Like the apostles, Paul didn't acquire fame, wealth, or power as a result of his evangelism. Instead, he gave up all his worldly privilege – his property, status, social standing, and more. And what did he get in return? Relentless persecution.

Paul faced more than his share of adversity – beatings, shipwrecks, hunger, imprisonment, stoning, angry mobs, exhaustion, sleepless nights, flogging, and other hardships. On one occasion, after Paul had preached the Good News to the people of Lystra, some Jews from Antioch and Iconium dragged him out of the city, stoned him, and left him for dead. But do you know what Paul did? He stood up and went right back into the city to preach (*Acts 14:19-20*). Is that what you would do? Again, why would he do this? What did he have to gain?

Ultimately, he was beheaded for his persistent preaching of the Gospel. Yet for years and years, up until his very last breath, Paul told everyone he came into contact with about the Messiah, Jesus Christ.

Paul's conversion had an enormous impact on my personal beliefs about Jesus. If what he saw on the road to Damascus was a lie, what was the motive? Why would he lie about such a thing, and then back up his lie with an unrelenting commitment to evangelism? Why would he preach and preach and preach in exchange for beatings, stonings, imprisonment, hunger, and eventual execution? He'd have to be crazy, and in reading his letters to the early churches, Paul appears to be anything but crazy. In fact, he was a man of sound mind and great eloquence – and as far as I can tell, neither one is a trademark characteristic of the insane.

The Actions of God's Witnesses

So what does all this mean? It means if you're truly objective, you need to admit that the early followers of Jesus offer powerful and credible testimony in support of His resurrection. Yes, throughout history many people have given their lives for false messiahs, but Jesus' followers were different. They abandoned Him in His hour of need. They saw Him die. They mourned. And *then*, they gave their lives. They weren't deluded by a charismatic leader, and they weren't part of a vast conspiracy. Those scenarios just don't make sense. Only one does — they saw the real God of the Universe.

These eyewitnesses faced persecution, torture, and death for their continued insistence that Jesus was who He said He was. In return, they received neither fame, fortune, nor worldly power over others. So why did they do it?

Furthermore, if Jesus and His followers were deluded, shouldn't there be evidence? Instead, everywhere I look, I see just the opposite. Fulfilled Old Testament prophecies indicate Jesus was the Messiah. His miracles testify that He was the Messiah, and countless men (even once mortal enemies) gave up everything to profess that Jesus was the Messiah, and they did this even though the result was nothing but persecution and eventual execution.

Examining the testimony of these eyewitnesses satisfied many of my original questions. *Is there a God?* Yes. There is a God. *And if so, who is He?* He's the God of Abraham, Isaac, and Jacob, and He answers to the name of Jesus. These facts I now knew for certain, but alone they didn't provide answers to all of my questions.

Yes, Jesus is Lord. *But does He care about you and me?* That was a question I definitely wanted to answer. Fortunately, I found that answer, and it was beyond anything I ever considered possible.

CHAPTER 8
WHAT HAPPENS WHEN YOU DIE

"And they sang in a mighty chorus: 'Worthy is the Lamb who was slaughtered — to receive power and riches and wisdom and strength and honor and glory and blessing.'"

— Revelation 5:12 (NLT)

ONCE I CONCLUDED the Bible was God's Word and Jesus was the Messiah, I had answers to many of my original questions. But several still remained. In fact, without answers to two questions in particular, I had to wonder if any of it mattered at all. What were those questions? Quite simply, I needed to know:

Does God care about me? And what will happen when I die?

And once I answered the second, I had the answer to the first.

The Bible says when you die, there are two destinations – and two destinations only. You either go to heaven or hell (***Romans 2:6-8***). But what determines where you end up? Before I reveal what the Bible says, let me ask you a question: Do "good" people get into heaven?

Even if you think you know the answer, take the time to think about that for a minute. If there's a heaven and a hell – and the Bible says there is – who goes to heaven and who goes to hell?

A lot of people are quick to answer this question. The common response is "good" people go to heaven and "bad" people go to hell. But this raises its own questions. Because if that's the case, where do you draw the line between "good" and "bad," and who sets the standard?

Getting Into Heaven

Someone once told me a story about a man who argued with a minister over this very question. He was convinced "good" people go to heaven and "bad" people go to hell. The minister asked the man if he viewed himself as one of the "good" people who would enter heaven. When the man said yes, the minister pulled out a sheet of paper. He drew a line from one side to the next. At one end, he wrote "0%" and at the other "100%."

"If God asked you to grade yourself on a scale of bad to good," he asked. "With 0% being totally evil and 100% being perfect in God's eyes – where would you put yourself?" The man thought for a minute or two, then put a "X" on the line at about the 75% mark.

Not bad. In fact, that's pretty good. Unfortunately, it's not good enough. God doesn't grade on a curve.

If you believe you're able to get into heaven because you've "lived a good life" or because you seem to be good by the world's standards, you're making a serious error. Why do I say this? Because such a belief is completely at odds with what the Bible says.

That's right. The same divinely inspired book which predicted the rise and fall of ancient empires and the coming of the Messiah with 100% accuracy. The same book quoted by Jesus and heralded by Paul as "fit for all reproof and instruction" (*2 Timothy 3:16*) says that no man is "good" – not even *one* (*Romans 3:10-12*).

So we have a problem here, don't we? According to God's Word, mankind is a fallen species, and no man is "good enough" to enter heaven on his own. Not one. That includes Gandhi, Mother Theresa, the Dalai Lama, and Billy Graham. It includes you, me, and even your kindly old grandmother who hasn't missed church in 95 years. In short, God's standard for entry into heaven is perfection, and every single one of us falls short. Since

God's requirement for entering heaven is absolute perfection, if you grade out anywhere less than 100% on that scale (and there's no cheating here – God knows what your true grade is ☺), then you're in trouble.

WHY THERE'S A PROBLEM

So why is all of mankind unworthy of entrance into heaven? To find out why, we need to go all the way back to the Garden of Eden. When Adam and Eve ate the forbidden fruit, they disobeyed God and broke His law. In other words, they sinned (*1 John 3:4*). When you sin, God turns away from you (*Isaiah 59:2*), because God is holy and cannot stand the sight of evil (*Habakkuk 1:13*). Since that moment in the Garden of Eden, sin has infected every one of us. We're born with it, generation after generation. And there's nothing we can do to get rid of it on our own. It's simply part of our nature. Do you see the problem here?

Because you are born into sin, you can't help but break God's law. You do it without thinking. So in the eyes of God, you and every single one of us is lost. The Bible says, the wages of sin is death (*Romans 6:23*). And because we are all sinners, every last one of us is condemned to die in our sins. And that means, outside of a miracle, we're all destined for hell – eternal separation from God.

"But wait!" you might say, "If no one on earth is good enough to enter heaven, then who can get in?"

That's a good question. By himself, not one person on this earth can get into heaven. Why? Because we're sinners. All of us. But don't worry. Before you hang your head in despair, I've got good news! The situation isn't hopeless. There has been a miracle. God *does* love us, and from the beginning of time He recognized this problem. And guess what? Loving God that He is, He devised a solution.

THE ULTIMATE SACRIFICE

Every year, on Easter weekend, our family watches Cecil B. DeMille's 1956 epic *The Ten Commandments*. One scene that always stands out for me is when God sends a plague of death to kill all the firstborn of Egypt. Only those households with lamb's blood above the door and on the doorposts escape unharmed (*Exodus 12*). While the Hollywood version isn't completely faithful to the biblical account – in this instance, it is.

So why did the blood of a lamb save the Israelites from death's grip? According to God, it is blood given in exchange for a life that makes purification possible (*Leviticus 17:11*). So when a lamb is sacrificed, its blood is a symbol of God reconciling Himself with man.

This is why God's people performed animal sacrifices in the Old Testament (*Exodus 29:36-39*). But we can't bridge the gap between ourselves and a Holy God through animal sacrifices. So what are we supposed to do?

Fortunately for us, God developed a perfect and permanent plan for dealing with our sin and the separation it creates between ourselves and Him. So what is this perfect plan? It's one sacrifice for the atonement of all sin (*Zechariah 9:11*). Did you get that? Not an endless, open-ended commitment to animal sacrifices in a Temple. But one sacrifice with everlasting consequences. That one sacrifice, the perfect lamb was the Messiah – Jesus Himself.

Animal sacrifice, along with many other Old Testament events, simply foreshadowed this ultimate sacrifice. For instance, as a test of faith, God commanded Abraham to sacrifice his only son Isaac (*Genesis 22:1-18*). Would you sacrifice your only child if God asked you? Abraham was willing, and his story foreshadowed God's willingness to sacrifice His one and only Son for you and me (*John 3:16*).

Three thousand years ago in Egypt, the lamb's blood saved the lives of those who were marked – just as the blood of Jesus saves us. This was God's plan from the very beginning. To sacrifice a perfect lamb in order to forgive the sins of the world. That perfect lamb was Jesus Christ. Jesus lived a sinless life. Yet He died a criminal's death on the cross for you and me.

WHAT THIS MEANS FOR YOU

So what does this mean for you? It means a definitive answer to a question you've probably asked at some point in your life. It's the same question I asked.

Does God care about me?

At this point, I hope the answer is clear. Yes. God cares about you and me and every human being who has ever lived. The evidence? God gave His only Son as a sacrifice to atone for our sins. He paid a ransom to save us from the empty, sinful life we inherited from Adam and Eve, and He didn't pay that ransom with cash, precious metals, or any other worldly treasure. He paid it with the blood of Jesus shed on the cross (*1 Peter 1:18-19*). The same Jesus the Old Testament prophets reveal as the Messiah – the sinless, spotless Lamb of God.

This is why John the Baptist called Jesus, "the lamb of God who takes away the sin of the whole world" (*John 1:29*). When Jesus was crucified on the eve of Passover, His death on the cross fulfilled the entire purpose of the Passover Lamb. The blood of Christ reconciles man with God. Did you know that? I didn't.

Growing up, I saw crosses everywhere. In front of churches. On walls. Everywhere. But I never really knew what the cross stood for. Sure, I knew a cross was a symbol for Jesus. But until I became a Christian, I never truly understood. I never "got it." But once I learned the truth, I realized just how much God cares about *me*. And you know what? He did the same thing for *you*. Don't believe me? If you have any doubts, I think they'll fade away forever when you read a love letter sent by God.

GOD'S LOVE LETTER

The Book of Isaiah was written over 700 years before the crucifixion. In fact, archaeologists date the oldest known complete copy of the Book of Isaiah to somewhere between 300 B.C. and 100 B.C. That's important to note, because it means what I'm about to show you isn't a case of back-dated material or historical revision. In Isaiah chapter 53, God wrote a love letter to you.

In fact, His message is so important I'm going to quote it right here in its entirety. After spending this whole book intentionally avoiding direct biblical quotes so you'll have to look them up yourself, I'm going to break my own rule. Why? Because I don't want to take a chance you won't actually read it. That's how important it is.

Here it is, courtesy of the New Living Translation:

"Who has believed our message? To whom has the Lord revealed his powerful arm? My servant grew up in the Lord's presence like a tender green shoot, like a root in dry ground. There was nothing beautiful or majestic about his appearance, nothing to attract us to him. He was despised and rejected — a man of sorrows, acquainted with deepest grief. We turned our backs on him and looked the other way. He was despised, and we did not care.

Yet it was our weaknesses he carried; it was our sorrows that weighed him down. And we thought his troubles were a punishment from God, a punishment for his own sins! But he was pierced for our rebellion, crushed for our sins. He was beaten so we could be whole. He was whipped so we could be healed. All of us, like sheep, have strayed away. We have left God's paths to follow our own. Yet the Lord laid on him the sins of us all.

He was oppressed and treated harshly, yet he never said a word. He was led like a lamb to the slaughter. And as a sheep is silent before the shearers, he did not open his mouth. Unjustly condemned, he was led away. No one cared that he died without descendants, that his life was cut short in midstream. But he was struck down for the rebellion of my people. He had done no wrong and had never deceived anyone. But he was buried like a criminal; he was put in a rich man's grave.

But it was the Lord's good plan to crush him and cause him grief.

Yet when his life is made an offering for sin, he will have many descendants. He will enjoy a long life, and the Lord's good plan will prosper in his hands. When he sees all that is accomplished by his anguish, he will be satisfied. And because of his experience, my righteous servant will make it possible for many to be counted righteous, for he will bear all their sins. I will give him the honors of a victorious soldier, because he exposed himself to death. He was counted among the rebels. He bore the sins of many and interceded for rebels." **Isaiah 53** (NLT)

Notice anything familiar? Sounds like a detailed description of Jesus, doesn't it? So much so you could easily mistake this for an excerpt from one of Paul's letters or a narrative from one of the four Gospel accounts of Jesus. But it's not. It's a passage from the Book of Isaiah – a book written more than 700 years before the crucifixion of Jesus.

I'll pause for a moment while that sinks in. The Book of Isaiah was written *seven centuries* before the life, death, and resurrection of Jesus Christ. More than 700 years before He was silent before His accusers. More than 700 years before He was buried in a rich man's tomb. More than 700 years before God laid the sins of the world upon Him.

And before you suggest that Christians edited or rewrote the Book of Isaiah after the crucifixion, keep in mind that the Jewish people have meticulously preserved it for 27 centuries. The Jews read the same chapter 53 of Isaiah that Christians read, and it points directly to Jesus.

Still wavering on the idea that Jesus is the Messiah? If you had any lingering doubts, I hope this passage permanently puts them to rest.

JESUS IS THE WAY

Think of it this way. Imagine you're standing before a judge. You've just been convicted of murder, and the mandatory penalty under law is death. You're condemned!

But before the bailiff removes you from court, your own father stands up and tells the judge he will take your place. The judge reads the letter of the law, which states only that a penalty of death must be paid. It says nothing about who must pay it, so he sets you free and takes your father into custody in preparation for execution.

While this is highly unlikely to occur in a modern courtroom, it's a perfect description of what Jesus did for us. It illustrates why Jesus is the only way to heaven. By accepting the penalty (death) for our conviction (sin), Jesus sets us free. That's why there's only one way to heaven. Only the blood of Jesus can set us free.

Many people disagree. "No," they say. "There are many paths to heaven."

We want to believe that. But this way of thinking contradicts everything Jesus and the Bible tell us. And after all we've learned about the credibility of Jesus and the Bible, do you really think it's wise to bet against them?

Jesus said, "I am the way and the truth and the life. No one comes to the Father except through me" (*John 14:6*). Read that again. No one. Not some or a few. *No one.* Were it not for the cross, there would be no hope for mankind.

Jesus knew He would bear the sins of the world at His crucifixion. He knew His sacrifice would be the only hope for our reconciliation with God. One sacrifice and one only – for all men.

This is what Jesus says, and He's clear about it. Yet some people get mad if you tell them there's only one path to heaven. Why? Why should anyone get angry when you tell them there's a path to heaven? Shouldn't they be excited? They should be. But all too often, they're not. Why?

More often than not, it's because they don't like that path, and they want to go their own way. They want all roads to lead to heaven so they're free to choose any path they want and still be able to convince themselves that it doesn't matter in the end.

So claiming there's only one way makes some people defensive, angry, and resentful. But why? If you don't believe there's only one way, why do you care if someone else does? If they're wrong, who cares what they think?

On the flip side, if you're open to the idea that there's only one way, then shouldn't you be grateful that there's even *one* way? You should. So why the push back?

I think it's because deep inside people realize it's possible there's only one way, but they're totally closed to the idea of taking it. In other words, if we're mad because God created only one path to heaven, we're not really upset because there's only one path. We're upset because we don't want to take it.

But what if God had closed the door to heaven all together? What if there was *no* path to heaven? Then life would truly be hopeless, right? Yet surprisingly few people ever look at it this way.

MANY PATHS TO HEAVEN?

One afternoon in my freshman college dorm room, one of the guys on our hall knocked on the door. "Hey, man," he said. "We're talking about God, and we want you to join us." This isn't something you hear every day, so I followed him a few doors down where four students were playing video games. They were also engaged in a deep conversation about what religion (if any) was "the true religion." Once I entered the room, the questions came from every direction.

"You're a Christian, right? Why do you believe that? Do you think non-Christians are going to hell?"

I explained that I believed Jesus was the way and the truth and the life and that no one could get into heaven except through Him. Only one of the four seemed to be bothered by this. He said he believed in Taoism, and while he admired Jesus and viewed Him as a great teacher, he found the narrow view of salvation through the cross as "too exclusive."

In his mind, there simply couldn't be only one way to heaven. There had to be many ways. How could any God, if He's really just, condemn someone to hell for growing up in a culture devoid of Christianity or for living in the backwoods where he had never heard the name of Jesus Christ? And what about the people who were born before Jesus?

Then came the question I've heard many times since… "Well Gandhi wasn't a Christian. Is he going to hell?" Of course, the insinuation is that

Gandhi was a "good person." Would God send a "good person" to hell simply for the crime of not being Christian? But this line of reasoning misses the mark.

I'm not here to stand in judgment of Gandhi or anyone else. I've never claimed a position of judgment over the souls of men. That's a judgment that belongs to Jesus Christ alone. But I can tell you this… If Gandhi or anyone else is in heaven, they got there *only* through the blood of Jesus Christ as shed on the cross.

There are many paths to the cross, but the cross is the only path to heaven. And whether or not you accept what Jesus did for you on the cross determines your destination when you die. Nothing else. Some people find that hard to accept because so many people openly reject Jesus. They ask, "Would a loving God send anyone to hell?" No. He wouldn't. What they fail to realize is that people send themselves to hell. Yes. Hell is a choice – a choice people make all the time. Because God laid down His life to keep us out of hell. So you literally have to trample over His dead body to get there.

WHAT HAPPENS WHEN YOU DIE

According to the Bible, there are only two possible destinations when you die – heaven and hell. And whether you end up in one or the other has nothing to do with what you've done and everything to do with God's grace. It's through faith alone that you get into heaven, not good works. The Bible tells us Abraham received salvation through faith (*Galatians 3:6*), and the faith of a thief crucified beside Jesus insured his salvation. When the thief said to Jesus, "Remember me in your kingdom," Jesus assured him they would walk together in paradise that day (*Luke 23:40-43*). If you have that type of faith, then you too will one day walk in paradise with Jesus.

No deed you perform on your own can gain you access to heaven, and a lifetime of charitable acts and self-sacrifice cannot erase even one sin. Your good deeds are worthless in the face of death. Entry into heaven is a gift pre-purchased with the blood of Jesus Christ. All you have to do is accept it.

Knowing that, you have a choice. Remember, God's price of admission into heaven is perfection. Are you perfect? Let me ask you this. Have you ever told a lie? If so, you broke God's law (***Exodus 20:16***). Have you ever stolen anything? If so, you broke another of His laws (***Exodus 20:15***). Have you ever lusted in your heart? If so, Jesus says you're guilty of adultery (***Matthew 5:28***). And if you're guilty of just one sin in your entire life, the Bible says you're guilty of breaking the whole law (***James 2:10***).

So what are you going to do? Try to cover up your guilt with good deeds? It might make you feel better for a little while. But how will those good deeds erase the bad ones? There's only one choice. If you want to enter heaven, you need the blood of Jesus to blot out your sin for all time. Without His blood, you're naked in your imperfection. With it, you're perfect in the eyes of God.

ANSWERS FOUND

In the Bible, I found the answers I was looking for. I now know what will happen when I die. I'm going to go straight to heaven and enter the presence of Jesus – just like the faithful thief on the cross. And why is this possible? It's only possible through the blood of Jesus Christ.

The power of the cross is the power of salvation. Without it, my life and your life are empty vessels. Don't believe me? Look around you. So many people are filled with emptiness. Why? Because they don't have Jesus in their hearts. That's why there's so much divorce and drug abuse and depression. Unhappy people tell themselves that their unhappiness is the result of what's around them. They think a new car, a new house, or a new spouse will bring happiness. But it never does. And the reason is simple. The problem isn't what's around us. It's what's in us. There's a void in every human heart, and only Jesus can fill it.

Is it any wonder I felt so empty all those years ago? Jesus was missing from my life, and His absence left a void in my heart. But once I welcomed Him in, He transformed my life in amazing ways. And if the same thing hasn't happened to you already, let me share with you just how that's possible. Because, believe it or not, Jesus can do the same thing for you ***right now***.

CHAPTER 9
PEACE AND LIFE PURPOSE

"I am leaving you with a gift – peace of mind and heart. And the peace I give is a gift the world cannot give. So don't be troubled or afraid."

— John 14:27 (NLT)

REMEMBER WHEN I said I used to look in the mirror as a child and wonder, "Who am I? And why am I me?" These were perplexing questions I couldn't answer, questions that filled me with emptiness. Before I uncovered the truth about Jesus, I would regularly ask myself questions just like this. Questions like: *Why do I exist? And what's the purpose of life?*

Most likely, you've considered these questions yourself. After all, who hasn't? The problem is most people are still searching for answers to those questions. But me? I found them.

WHAT'S THE PURPOSE OF LIFE?

Let's start with the purpose of life. What is it? Is it to indulge in fleeting pleasures? To accumulate "stuff"? The world would have us believe it is. Have you ever heard the slogan, "He who dies with the most toys wins"? I've known quite a few people over the years who think that statement is true. That's the world's slogan, and it's a philosophy that leads to destruction. You'll never find your true purpose or have lasting peace in your life making the pursuit of wealth or pleasure your god.

How can I be so sure? Because the basic needs of the human heart are the same for people throughout the world. We're all looking for answers to the same questions. Only some people don't know what they're looking for. But have no doubt, the whole world is searching for something. You can use any number of words to describe it. You can call it purpose, meaning, or fulfillment. But Pascal described it best – we all have a God-shaped vacuum in our hearts, and we're looking to fill it with something.

Some people look for it in sex, drugs, and rock and roll. Others in the pursuit of wealth, fame, and other worldly pleasures. Some even seek it through good deeds or charitable work. Yet, they never find the purpose or the peace they're searching for. It's never enough. And it never will be. Why? One simple reason. Only Jesus can fill that God-shaped vacuum.

Don't believe me? Think of the kings of past centuries who lived lives of opulent luxury. Those same lives would be considered poverty when compared to the life *you* live today. Did I just say you? Yes, I did. You. Not Bill Gates or Warren Buffett. You. Even though you may not consider yourself wealthy, you probably live a life of luxury that would make past world rulers green with envy.

For instance, you're probably reading this book on a mobile e-reader device, a virtual library in the palm of your hand. The elite and wealthy of past centuries could only dream of such a thing!

They yearned for what you have – an iPod that puts a symphony in your ear, music and entertainment on demand, accelerated travel, smart phones, temperature-controlled pools, hot and cold running water, life saving medicine, surgical procedures, abundant food, water on demand, and thousands of food choices with different spices and flavors. The list goes on and on. We could fill an entire book with a list of items you have that they desired.

The kings and queens of the past thought they would have peace and satisfaction if they acquired these things. But you have them. And guess what? You still want more. Don't you?

In fact, you probably repeatedly tell yourself, "I'll be much happier when…" I get that job, promotion, house, car, or inheritance. Or I'll be much happier when I'm married, have a baby, or move to that beautiful city.

Yet no matter what you achieve or acquire, it's never enough, is it? And if you haven't figured it out by now, I've got news for you – it never will be. Yes, more stuff will make you happy (so you think), and sometimes you enjoy the illusion of happiness for a short time. But it's nothing more than that – a passing illusion. You will only find the lasting peace and contentment you're looking for in one place. And that's Jesus Christ. Everything else is as meaningless as chasing the wind (*Ecclesiastes 1:14*).

Unfortunately, too many people never figure this out. They live an entire lifetime devoid of real purpose and meaning, just going through the motions of life. They follow a path that appears to be right, but in the end, it only leads to death and destruction (*Proverbs 14:12*).

So how do you find purpose in life? King Solomon, one of the wisest men who ever lived, asked himself this same question. His conclusion? The purpose of life is to fear God and obey His commands, for the judgment is coming (*Ecclesiastes 12:13-14*).

And what did Solomon mean when he said this? He meant that all the pleasures and achievements of this world are fleeting and meaningless. All that matters is your relationship with God and the coming judgment. All else pales in comparison.

So if you want purpose and peace in your life, you need to put aside your own selfish desires and ambitions (*Luke 9:23*). You need to reconcile with God and seek His purpose for your life.

GOD'S PLAN FOR YOU

Everyone wants to live a life of purpose. And everyone can live that life in Jesus Christ. Jesus said His purpose is to give a rich and satisfying life to all who come to Him (*John 10:9-10*). When you embrace the truth about Jesus, not only do you experience liberation and freedom, but you also receive an infusion of life purpose. The Bible says that God calls people and gives them a purpose (***Romans 8:28***).

Even if you don't know what they are yet, God has great plans for you. Plans for good, not evil. Plans to give you hope and a future (***Jeremiah 29:11***). So how do you discover God's specific purpose for your life? Start with what Jesus said we should all be doing. First, love the Lord your God with all your heart, soul, mind, and strength. And second, love your neighbor as yourself (***Mark 12:30-31***). When you do these things, you will become more and more Christ-like, and along the way, God will reveal His specific plan for your life.

Need another idea for finding your life purpose? Maybe you're already doing these things, but you're still struggling to understand God's plan for your life? If so, here's a radical idea – ask. That's right. ***Ask***. Talk to God and ask Him to reveal His purpose for your life. His timing may be different from yours, but if you're persistent, He will answer you. Jesus said, "Ask and you shall receive" (***Matthew 7:7***). So ask.

In Jesus, every life has purpose. And when you know your life has purpose, the cares of this world fade away – replaced by an overwhelming sense of freedom, peace, and contentment. This is the exact opposite of what the world tells you.

According to the world, you're a nobody unless you have fame, wealth, power, talent, nice clothes, and more. But this is the world's way of thinking. Look around. Plenty of people have those things, and yet many of them are absolutely miserable. Why? Because true, long-term contentment comes not from the accumulation of worldly "things," but from knowing Jesus.

If you don't have the attributes championed by this world, then the world may not think much of you. But in God's eyes you are the most important person in the world. He doesn't care about your station in life or what the people of this world think about you.

In the eyes of the world, a blind beggar living in abject poverty is a nobody – certainly not someone who drew the best lot in life. But the world's ways are not God's ways. In God's world, a blind beggar given sight by the Son of God (***John 9:1-34***) is a life of great fame and wealth, bringing glory to the God of Israel. It's a life of eternal significance. If you aren't familiar with this story, I encourage you to read it now. God infused that blind beggar's life with real purpose – so much so that you and I remember him to this day.

And just as God had a purpose for the blind beggar, He has a purpose for you as well. Regardless of what you or the world may think, **you** are important. Why? Because God loves you. Not only did He offer His only Son as a sacrifice to redeem you from your sins, but He offers the very Spirit of Jesus to live within you (**Romans 8:11**). He knows your thoughts, your motives, and your desires. And He has an amazing plan for your life – a plan for a full life filled with joy and contentment.

Your life is extremely meaningful, and God designed a specific purpose for it before you were ever born (**Jeremiah 1:5**). God's plan is for you to know Him – to live for Him and enjoy His presence every day.

So infuse your life with purpose and energy by living the way He wants you to, by worshipping Him, and by sharing the Good News of Jesus with others. Bring Him glory. The same as the blind beggar (**John 9:3**), and the same as the paralytic (**John 5:8-9**).

As a unique individual, created by God for a specific purpose, your job is simple – to serve God and those around you by utilizing the unique talents and resources He gave you. Shine with the light of Christ in your life. Work like you're working for Jesus. Raise your children like you're raising them for Jesus. Show kindness to a stranger as if Jesus Himself is the stranger. Share His light with the world, and you will feel the Spirit of God working through you. And His Spirit will give you peace.

A LIFE OF PEACE

In Jesus, you will find fullness of joy (**Psalm 16:11**), and knowing your purpose, you will receive a peace the world does not understand. Through Christ, you can combat sickness, depression, despair, addiction, loneliness, anger, and unhappiness. If you feel crushed by stress, worry, tension, anxiety, fear, lack of money, or massive debt, Jesus can give you new life. Because you'll soon come to realize that all these things are temporary. Only your soul is eternal, and it's in His hands. God is in control. What freedom in knowing your eternal destiny lies in the hands of someone who loves you so much!

When you know the truth about Jesus, it breeds faith, hope, and courage. You have a passion for life which escapes others. If you belong to Jesus, there's no need to worry. You're not condemned, and because you belong to Him, His Spirit frees you from death in your sins (**Romans 8:1-2**). For where the Spirit of the Lord resides, there is freedom (**2 Corinthians 3:17**).

Let the power of Jesus work through you. Boast in your weakness and imperfection. Take pleasure in the insults, hardships, pains, and troubles you suffer for Him. For when you are weak, then you are strong (**2 Corinthians 12:9-10**). Experience the freedom of Christ in the face of the world's troubles, because when you belong to Jesus, none of the worries of this world can crush you. You'll know the truth of Christ's victory, and the truth will set you free (**John 8:32**). Jesus invited all who are weary, all who carry heavy burdens, to come to Him. He promised them rest. "Let me teach you," He said, "and you will find rest for your soul" (**Matthew 11:28-30**).

So many people suffer needlessly under the weight of worry, guilt, or fear. If they would only take Jesus at His word, believing that everything will work out to His purpose, they would feel a heavy weight lifted from their shoulders.

To illustrate, imagine you're hiking up the side of a steep mountain, and you're weighed down with a heavy backpack. Accompanying you up the side of the mountain is a friendly giant who offers to carry your backpack for you. Are you going to turn him down? That's exactly what you do when you choose to shoulder your own burdens rather than giving them to Jesus. Jesus is more than able to carry anything that weighs you down, so put your faith in Him, and He will take that burden from your shoulders.

When you understand Jesus is in control, you stop worrying so much. You know you're never alone, because you're safely in His hands forever. This is the peace only Jesus can give. It's a feeling that exceeds anything you can understand, and it will overrun your heart and mind as you live for Him (**Philippians 4:6-7**). This peace comes only from knowing you are reconciled with God because of what Jesus did for you on the cross (**Romans 5:1**). Jesus promised to leave us His peace as a gift, and it's a peace the world cannot offer (*John 14:27*).

Just look around you. Many of us live unsettled, tempestuous lives burdened with worry and anxiety for the future. Our life problems create a world filled with stress, fear, and regret. But with Jesus, we're better equipped to deal with the problems of this world. They don't go away, but they no longer seem overwhelming. Trials and tribulations will always be a part of life, and Jesus warned that we will have many. But we don't have to worry or be afraid, because He has overcome the world (*John 16:33*).

WHAT JESUS OFFERS

While much of the world lives in dread and despair, Jesus offers you peace and rest. Do you have peace in your life?

I do. Once I put my trust in Jesus, the emptiness that consumed my life melted away. I now live a life of total peace and contentment. Sure, I face frustrations and obstacles. I get irritated like anyone else. But I know these are just speed bumps in the road of life. Through it all, I'm confident I can handle *anything* that life throws my way. Can you say that? If not, come to Jesus and receive His rest.

The world can take away my wife, my kids, my home, my health, all the money in my bank account, and every possession I have. But it will not destroy me. The entire universe and the gates of hell can be aligned against me – but I'll be fine. Because nothing can take Jesus from my life. He's the same yesterday, today, and tomorrow (*Hebrews 13:8*). I've built my life on an unmovable rock, and He gives me peace. Can you say that? If not, come to Jesus and He will give you that same peace.

I can deal with any circumstance (*Philippians 4:11-13*), no matter how dire, because the foundation and purpose of my life is Jesus. And nothing can shake that foundation. Serve another master – fame, money, power, or even good deeds – and eventually you'll be destroyed by the storms of life. But I know nothing can separate me from the love of Jesus Christ. I am His follower, created in His image. And I am me so that I can bring honor and glory to His name.

I know why I'm here. I know what my purpose is, and I know where I'm going when I die. Can you say that? If not, come to Jesus so He can give you the same assurance.

An eternity of freedom and joy, confident in the knowledge of your unique purpose is right in front of you. It can begin in your life right now. All you have to do is take it. Will you? If you want, you can begin your new life right now. All you have to know is *how*.

And fortunately for you, I have the answer.

CHAPTER 10
DEVELOPING A PERSONAL RELATIONSHIP WITH JESUS CHRIST

"My sheep listen to my voice; I know them, and they follow me."

— John 10:27 (NLT)

D O YOU KNOW Jesus? I mean really ***know*** Him? Even if you've been confirmed, baptized, or sat in a church pew every Sunday for the past 50 years, it doesn't mean you know Him. There's a big difference between "being religious" or identifying with your family's Christian heritage and actually trusting in and relying on Jesus Christ in your day-to-day life.

Remember, a person is not righteous in God's eyes because of water baptism, good works, or fancy ceremonies in the presence of other people. You're only counted as righteous because of your faith in Him. Think I'm wrong? Go read the story of the thief on the cross (***Luke 23:40-43***). There's no evidence he was ever baptized or that he ever attended synagogue or even read the scriptures. Yet, Jesus promised him this – "Today, you will walk with me in paradise."

No sermons. No chants. No special ceremonies. No advanced knowledge or memorization of scriptures. Just faith. This man's faith in Jesus allowed him to enter heaven because it clothed him in the redeeming blood of Jesus Christ. If you want to join them both in heaven when you die, Jesus is the only way. Jesus says, "I am the way and the truth and the life. No one comes to the Father except through me" (*John 14:6*).

But Jesus offers more than just a ticket to heaven. He offers you a new life. I can personally testify to that. Once I put my trust in Jesus, Pascal's God-shaped vacuum disappeared from my life. It's been years and years since I last experienced the dread and emptiness that accompanies it. Can you say the same? If not, take action today. If you desire to have a personal relationship with Jesus, here are the steps you need to take.

#1: Admit You're a Sinner – Before you can be reconciled with God, you need to admit you're a sinner in need of a Savior. Don't let pride stop you. We're all sinners. We all fall short of the glory of God (*Romans 3:23*), and our sin separates us from Him.

Once you acknowledge your sins, recognize them as poor choices and turn to God for direction in your life. This is what people mean when they say you need to "repent." To repent means you change your mind about sin. As Peter explains, to receive the Holy Spirit, you must repent of your sins and turn to God (*Acts 2:38*).

#2: Believe in Jesus – The Bible says if you confess with your mouth that Jesus Christ is Lord, and believe in your heart that God raised Him from the dead, then you will not die in your sins (*Romans 10:9*). And Peter says to rely on the blood of Jesus Christ as payment for your sins (*Acts 2:38*). If you desire a closer relationship with God, put your trust in Jesus. The Bible says anyone who believes in Him will not be disappointed (*Romans 10:11*).

#3: Pray to Receive Him – Once you've performed the first two steps, pray for Jesus to come into your life. Because of what Jesus did on the cross, if you believe in Him, you will receive His promised Holy Spirit through faith alone. As the very Spirit of Jesus Himself, the indwelling presence of the Holy Spirit in your heart is how God identifies you as one who belongs to Him. It's a down payment from Jesus that guarantees everything He has promised (*2 Corinthians 1:21-22*).

If you're willing to take these simple steps, you can pray this prayer right now:

"Dear Jesus, have mercy on my soul, for I am a sinner. I repent of my sins, and I believe that you died on the cross as forgiveness for my sins. I invite you to come into my life. Fill my heart with your Spirit, and I will trust and follow you as my Lord and Savior. In the name of Jesus. Amen."

Say that prayer, and your sins are forgiven. The Bible says, all who call on the name of the Lord will be saved (***Romans 10:13***). So don't believe for a moment that God doesn't love you or that you need to wait until you're "living a better life" to take these steps. That's the devil speaking. The Holy Spirit is freely available for all who seek it. It's not in limited supply. It's not for an exclusive few. Jesus died for everyone, and not one person is out of reach of His saving grace. But you must be willing to ***receive*** this gift. He won't force it upon you.

So welcome Him. Don't hesitate for one moment to invite Jesus into your life. Jesus promised, "I am the resurrection and the life. Anyone who believes in me will live, even after dying. Everyone who lives in me and believes in me will never ever die" ***John 11:25-26*** (NLT).

What Happens Now?

If you decided to take these steps and commit your life to Jesus Christ, congratulations! Once you confess with your tongue and believe in your heart that Jesus died for your sins and rose from the dead, something amazing happens. God's Holy Spirit comes to reside ***in you*** – just as Jesus promised.

The Holy Spirit fills the void in your life. It literally breathes life into the walking dead. As Pascal noted, "There is a God-shaped vacuum in the heart of every person, and it can never be filled by any created thing. *It can only be filled by God.*"

According to the Bible, Jesus, the prophets, and the apostles – Jesus, God, and the Holy Spirit are one and the same. So when the Holy Spirit fills the God-shaped vacuum in your heart, it's a perfect fit. The emptiness within you is filled with God Himself.

That emptiness is gone because you're "born again." You've probably heard that phrase before. But what does it mean? While meeting with a man named Nicodemus, Jesus revealed that while your mother may give birth to your physical life, the Holy Spirit gives birth to your spiritual life. That's why He claimed you cannot see the Kingdom of God unless you are "born again" (*John 3:3-8*).

When the Holy Spirit enters your life, you experience a great transformation. You become a new creation, and the desires of your old life start to yield to the desires of Jesus. And when this happens, you experience a peace unlike anything you've ever felt. This process doesn't require a bolt of lightning or a dramatic Hollywood epiphany. Sometimes it's gradual, but it's quite noticeable. How can I be so sure it doesn't require a "bolt of lightning" moment?

Because as a loyal follower of Jesus Christ, I can honestly say I never had a "bolt of lightning" moment. I can't tell you the day or the hour I was born again. But I do know that it was sometime in late 1992 or early 1993.

I remember kneeling in front of my bedroom window and praying for Jesus to come into my life. Afterward, I didn't feel any different physically. But from that moment on, my life began to change. Over the course of the weeks and months that followed, everything changed – from what I thought was important in life to how I treated other people. Most importantly, a sense of peace entered my life which had never been there before.

Some people have a different experience. They can tell you the very day, hour, and even minute when they were born again. They describe their experience as an electrifying, transformative moment they'll never forget. That's great. But if that doesn't happen to you, don't worry. It doesn't necessarily mean the Holy Spirit isn't within you.

YOU WON'T BE PERFECT

Even as the Holy Spirit lives within you, you won't be perfect. I can tell you this from firsthand experience. My sophomore year in college, I started drinking on a regular basis. I wasn't an alcoholic, but like many college students, I allowed drinking to play a much larger role in my life than it should have. It's something I should never have allowed myself to become entangled with. But I did.

So why do I bring this up? Because many people (both Christians and non-Christians alike) live under a common misconception. They think Christians need to live perfect lives. But this isn't possible. We're all sinners, and while the blood of Jesus Christ saves you from death in your sins, accepting Jesus Christ as your Savior doesn't mean you become instantly transformed into a perfect being. So don't ever buy into that belief. You don't need to strive for perfection to be a Christian. Just get out of the way so He can live through you!

Think I'm wrong? Think God demands perfection? If so, take note of the following biblical heroes who lived less than perfect lives:

Noah was a righteous man who lived in close fellowship with God (*Genesis 6:9*), yet Noah got drunk (*Genesis 9:21*). The Bible says Abraham was counted righteous because of his faith (*Romans 4:22*), yet he refused to believe God's promise that his wife Sarah would bear a child, so he slept with her maidservant Hagar (*Genesis 16:1-4*). God called David a man after His own heart (*1 Samuel 13:14*), yet David committed adultery with Bathsheba and then plotted the murder of her husband to cover it up (*2 Samuel 11*). And Paul, who spread the Gospel of Jesus throughout the Roman Empire called himself "a slave to sin" who wants to do right, but doesn't always do it (*Romans 7:14-15*).

All these men were loved by God. And none of them were perfect. Likewise, He doesn't expect you to be perfect. Now, does that mean it's okay to sin if you're a Christian? Absolutely not. The Bible says you become a slave to whatever you choose to obey, and Christians should be slaves to Jesus, not slaves to sin (*Romans 6:15-16*).

Just like a newborn child, when we are born again, it takes time to grow to adulthood. Along the way, we will fall many times. But we should measure ourselves not by how many times we fall, but by how many times we get back up, moving forward as the Holy Spirit leads us to become more and more like Jesus.

One day, when you're in heaven, you'll be perfect. Until then, you're going to make mistakes. But if you confess your sins, He is faithful and will purify you from all unrighteousness (*1 John 1:9*). God doesn't expect you to be perfect. He expects you to trust Him, to believe in Jesus – the one He has sent (*John 6:29*). So if you're feeling unworthy, and it's holding you back, don't wait one moment longer to approach Him. The time for you to come to Him is *now*.

There's also another lesson here. Don't ever put your faith in others. Now when I say that I don't mean you should never trust a fellow human being. What I mean is that you should never look up to another Christian the way you should look up to Jesus. Don't put your faith in sinful humans. Don't put your faith in religious institutions, preachers, teachers, or any other human beings. Why? Because you will eventually be disappointed in all of them. Instead, put your faith in Jesus. Focus your attention on Him alone. He is the shining example you should follow.

Looking back, I'm glad for the mistakes I've made. My experience with alcohol made me a better person, because I now have a greater understanding of people who develop addictions to things like alcohol, drugs, gambling, and food. Before I started drinking, I probably lacked compassion for such people. But my personal experience with alcohol gave me new perspective. Instead of becoming someone who prayed, "Thank you God, that I am not like them," each day I pray, "God, I am a sinner. Have mercy on my soul." (*Luke 18:13*). Today, I no longer drink. But I thank God for the sins and struggles of my past, because they make me better able to relate to other people.

In fact, maybe *you're* one of those people. Do you struggle with alcohol? How about drugs? Gambling? Depression? Worry? No matter how big you may think your problem is, it isn't too big for Jesus. He can handle anything, even when all else has failed.

DEEPEN YOUR RELATIONSHIP

Once you've committed your life to Jesus Christ, don't just sit back and wait. Devote your life to glorifying His name. Discipline yourself like an athlete, training to do what you should (*1 Corinthians 9:25-27*). Strive to make Him master of every area of your life. The following activities are a good place to focus:

#1 Study – Read the Bible. It's the verifiable Word of God. It's His message to the world. If some parts seem boring, save them for later and read the parts that excite you. At first, you may not understand all of it, but that's okay.

If you're having trouble understanding, ask God for greater insight into His Word. For instance, people often ask me, "How did you know that? Where did you learn that? And how do you know so much about the Bible?"

While I certainly don't know everything about the Bible, people who ask me these questions seem astounded by how much I do know. And their questions are legitimate. After all, where *did* I learn the things I know? I didn't grow up in a church, and I can count on one hand the number of Sunday school classes I've ever attended. I've never set foot in a seminary or a biblical school of higher learning. So how did I acquire such a deep understanding of the scriptures, particularly when it comes to bible prophecy? The answer is really quite simple.

I asked. That's right. I asked.

I asked God for insight and understanding of His Word, and then I studied the Bible. Jesus promised, "Everyone who asks will receive, and everyone who seeks will find" (*Matthew 7:7-8*). I took Him at His word. I asked, and I received. And you can do the same. If you want to know more about God, it's quite simple – just ask Him.

#2 Pray – Prayer is essential to your relationship with Jesus. Talk to Him through prayer. The Bible says you should "devote yourself to prayer with an alert mind and a thankful heart" *Colossians 4:2* (NLT), and you should never stop praying (*1 Thessalonians 5:17*).

Now I know it may sound impossible to pray continuously. But when the Holy Spirit dwells within you, you can walk through life with your mind, body, and soul continually focused on Jesus and still carry out the daily tasks of life. This doesn't come through meditation or focusing your mind. It only comes when you surrender your life to Jesus.

#3 Evangelize – Jesus commanded us to spread the Good News about what He did for us. He said, "Go and make disciples of all men" (**Matthew 28:19**). If you're filled with the Holy Spirit, you will not be ashamed of Jesus or the message of the cross, and you'll leap at any opportunity to preach the Gospel (**Acts 1:8**).

Over the years, I haven't been able to stop myself from telling as many people as possible about the glory of Jesus Christ. I told them all the things I've told you so far in this book. I told them about the Bible's numerous fulfilled prophecies, including the Messianic prophecies fulfilled in the life of Jesus. I told them about the actions of the apostles and the transformation of Paul in a mere moment. Because of this, many people opened their hearts to the Gospel. So never hesitate to tell people about Jesus. The Bible says you should always be ready to give an account for why you believe (**1 Peter 3:15**).

#4 Worship – Jesus is worthy of our worship, and worship means more than just honoring Him with your lips (**Isaiah 29:13**). We should worship Jesus in spirit and truth (**John 4:21-24**). Give your body as a living, holy sacrifice. Don't conform to the ways of the world, but let God transform the way you think and live (**Romans 12:1-2**). Worship Him in praise and song (**Psalm 150:1-6**). Worship Him by being a light to the world (**Matthew 5:14-16**).

#5 Fellowship – Jesus said, "Whenever two or more gather in my name, I am there among them" (**Matthew 18:20**), and Paul said Christians should encourage each other and build each other up (**1 Thessalonians 5:11**). Following Jesus is not meant to be a solitary journey. So fellowship with other Christians. Go to church. Join groups of like-minded people who share your interest in learning more about God's Word. Encourage each other (**Romans 1:12**) and motivate each other (**Hebrews 10:24-25**).

#6 Serve – Jesus washed the feet of His disciples (**John 13:4-17**). He did this as an example of how we should serve others, so show your love for Jesus by serving others. Serve everyone you meet as if you're serving Jesus Himself. Because, according to Jesus, you **are** serving Him. Jesus said whenever you give a drink to someone who is thirsty or clothing to someone who is naked or kindness to someone who is sick or in prison – then you have done those things to Him (**Matthew 25:37-40**).

While good deeds can never redeem a sinner in God's eyes, if you love Jesus, you will gladly serve others. The Bible says "faith without good works is dead" (**James 2:26**). And Jesus said, "He who is first must be last" (**Mark 9:35**), meaning if you want to be a champion for Jesus, you need to humble yourself and become a servant to others.

Concluding Thoughts

Many years ago, as I lay in a hospital bed contemplating the universal questions of life – questions we've all asked, I had no idea what was in store for the future. Never in my wildest dreams did I imagine that the Creator of the Universe would reach out and tell me He loves me. Never did I imagine that He would answer all of my questions and reveal Himself in the way He did. Maybe you feel the same way right now, but I assure you, God will reveal Himself to you if only you let Him.

Lying in that hospital bed, I was completely ignorant of the hundreds of fulfilled bible prophecies pointing to Jesus as God of the Universe. I knew nothing about the testimony of the apostles, Paul's radical conversion, or the bold claim of Jesus to be God in the flesh. I knew nothing of the peace that only Jesus can bring. But I praise God that He opened my heart and revealed these things to me.

I've shared my story and just a few reasons I believe Jesus Christ is the Savior we all need, but you shouldn't take my word for it. Investigate the scriptures yourself. Put them to the test. Don't simply dismiss the Bible as an ancient text written by superstitious men until you read it for yourself. Read the Old Testament prophecies. In my opinion, fulfilled prophecy is undeniable proof that the God of Israel wrote the Bible. Maybe you disagree, but you'll never know for sure until you read and examine them for yourself. There's too much at stake to simply rely on the conclusions of others.

While this book may catalogue the path that led me to Jesus Christ, it's not about me. It's about *you*. It's about your life and the opportunity you have right now to know Him. At some point, you will decide the status of your relationship with the God of the Universe once and for all.

You have a choice, and it's the most important decision you will ever make. Will you accept the blood of Jesus as payment for your sins? Or will you take your chances on the day of judgment, relying on your own righteousness to save you? Believe me, those are the only two choices.

Sure, you can tell yourself you'll think about it. You can tell yourself you'll wait until later. But in the here and now, your procrastination is a choice. Despite what you may tell yourself, eventually time will force you to make a choice. And it may be a choice you regret. Don't let that happen. The time to know Him is *now*. There may not be a tomorrow.

Think about what's at stake – your eternal soul. You wouldn't buy a house and not get insurance, would you? What if there's a fire? You'd lose everything. Isn't your soul worth more than a house? The Bible says if you die without the redeeming blood of Jesus Christ, your final destination is hell. But with His blood, your final destination is heaven. If that's the case, why put your soul at risk when you won't even put your house at risk? Commit to Jesus today and secure His promise for eternity.

Remember, Solomon was one of the wisest men who ever lived, and he said nothing in all of life matters except this: *fear God and obey His commands, for the judgment is coming (**Ecclesiastes 12:13**).* Jesus Himself agreed, saying "What good will it do you to gain the whole world if you lose your own soul in the process?" (**Mark 8:36**). Don't spend your life in pursuit of temporary pleasure and satisfaction while ignoring the one thing that matters forever – your relationship with Him.

Right now, you can have peace through Jesus Christ. Right now, He is knocking on the door of your heart. Answer Him, and He promises to come into your life (***Revelation 3:20-21***). Will you answer? He's waiting. At this very moment, He's reaching out, and you may never again have the opportunity to answer Him. The Bible says what you already know in your heart – there's no guarantee of tomorrow (***James 4:14***). This could be your last chance to receive Him. So make your choice now.

All those years ago, I faced the same choice. I chose Jesus, and it was the greatest decision I ever made. I now have peace, joy, and truth in my life. I know why I'm here. I know what my purpose is, and I know where I'm going. Do you? If not, you can. But only if you make the same choice. So I encourage you – come to Him. Come to Jesus.

SHARE THE GOOD NEWS

The arguments on behalf of Jesus and the fulfilled bible prophecies cited in this book are nothing new. They're the same arguments the apostles used to evangelize the known world in the first century. The primary message of the early church was this: "The Messiah you are looking for is Jesus" (**Acts 5:42**). Peter and the apostles knew that fulfillment of the Messianic prophecies offered a powerful and persuasive testimony in favor of Jesus as Lord and Savior.

You can use these same concepts today to spread the Good News of Jesus Christ. I encourage you to do so. But maybe you struggle with words. If so, use this book to spread the Gospel.

Consider giving it as a gift. Do you have friends or family who have yet to know peace through Jesus Christ? Do you know others struggling with depression, addiction, loneliness, or fear of the unknown? If so, give them the best gift possible. Give them the Good News of Jesus!

ABOUT THE AUTHOR

Britt Gillette is a devoted follower of Jesus Christ, husband to Jen, and father to Samantha and Tommy. He and his family live in Virginia.

If you want to receive an automatic email when Britt's next book is released, please sign up on his website. Your email address will never be shared and you can unsubscribe at any time.

Spread the Word
Word-of-mouth is crucial for any book to succeed. If you enjoyed this book, please consider leaving a review at Amazon. Even if it's only a sentence or two, it would make a world of difference and would be very much appreciated.

Also, please consider using social media to share this book with others. Tell your Facebook friends, your Twitter followers, and others. You can make a difference in someone's life today by sharing the Good News of Jesus Christ.

Come Visit Us on the Web
Britt writes a number of articles about Jesus Christ and bible prophecy on his website, www.end-times-bible-prophecy.com. Please drop by and visit!

11979816R00069

Made in the USA
San Bernardino, CA
08 December 2018